PEOPLE Magazine on Tom Brown, Jr.

"Brown is a *tracker*, a practitioner of a skill that faded away with the frontier in this country. He stalks men and animals, mostly in the remote Pine Barrens of New Jersey but also as far afield as the Virgin Islands and Wyoming. Tom, 28, has found 40 missing persons and helped investigate four murders . . ."

Tom Brown, Jr., on STALKING WOLF

. . . Rick took me home with him to meet the man who was to be my teacher and guide for the next nine years. I was in awe of Stalking Wolf from the beginning. He was of medium height and lean, like his grandson Rick, but his features were classically Indian. His eyes seemed to be looking at things very far away . . .

THE TRACKER on Tracking

The first track is the end of a string. At the far end, a being is moving; a mystery, dropping a hint about itself every so many feet, telling you more about itself until you can almost see it, even before you come to it.

PORCUPINE

FOREFOOT

HIND FOOT

RUNNING

THE TRACKER

The Story of Tom Brown, Jr. as told to William Jon Watkins

A BERKLEY BOOK
published by
BERKLEY PUBLISHING CORPORATION

RED SQUIRREL · SITTING   SLOW LOPE

This Berkley book contains the complete
text of the original hardcover edition.
It has been completely reset in a type face
designed for easy reading, and was printed
from new film.

THE TRACKER

A Berkley Book / published by arrangement with
Prentice-Hall, Inc.

PRINTING HISTORY
Prentice-Hall edition published 1978
Berkley edition / November 1979

ISBN: 0–425–04222–7

A BERKLEY BOOK® TM 757,375
Berkley Books are published by Berkley Publishing Corporation,
200 Madison Avenue, New York, New York 10016.
PRINTED IN THE UNITED STATES OF AMERICA

To my wife, Judy, my daughter, Kelly, and my son, Paul, whom I love and cherish more than wild Nature itself.

In all potential and manifested universes, for Sandra, my first and last love; and for Tara, Wade, and Chad, the reincarnational players who make us a family.

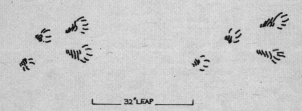

32" LEAP

OTTER · WALKING

Contents

viii

THE TRACKER

4⅞"

2½"

BARRED OWL IN MUD

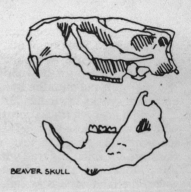

BEAVER SKULL

1/The Ultimate Track

The first track is the end of a string. At the far end, a being is moving; a mystery, dropping a hint about itself every so many feet, telling you more about itself until you can almost see it, even before you come to it. The mystery reveals itself slowly, track by track, giving its genealogy early to coax you in. Further on, it will tell you the intimate details of its life and work, until you know the maker of the track like a lifelong friend.

The mystery leaves itself like a trail of breadcrumbs, and by the time your mind has eaten its way to the maker of the tracks, the mystery is inside you, part of you forever. The tracks of every mystery you have ever swallowed move inside your own tracks, shading them slightly or skewing them with nuances that show how much *more* you have become than what you were.

Man goes through the world eating his mysteries. I

1

have followed every mystery I could in the twenty years since I began my apprenticeship with an old Apache tracker named Stalking Wolf. I have had no choice in this. Mysteries are irresistible to me, and a trail is something that *must* be followed until it gives up its secret or puts me onto the trail of something even more amazing. Tracks fascinate me.

I watch my own tracks constantly. They go like a dog with a curious nose always catching scent of something unidentifiable hovering just out of reach. If I go to the store for milk, my trail winds a quarter of a mile to go a block and a half. Even in a small New Jersey town, the landscape is as full of invisible animals as a child's puzzle.

One winter after a moderate snow, I went out to get milk and found the track of a small gray bird called a Junco. I like the silhouette of the Junco; its head rounds so smoothly into its back that it looks like it ought to be made out of chrome. Birds are always mysteries. They leave their track in the air most of the time and I don't have the nose to follow it. Their tracks on the ground were irresistible.

I crouched down and looked at them, judging the size and shape of the prints to get the type of bird. I watched its ease of movement on the ground and knew it wasn't a finch or a sparrow. The tracks went from seed to seed in an easy zig-zagging line. Looking close I could see where the bird had stopped and leaned a little to one side, breaking down the side of its print while it ducked and then craned its head up. I saw where it gave a little defensive hop as something that seemed threatening must have gone by overhead.

The movement from a hop to a better balanced stance said there had been danger. The way the toes went into the snow and curled under told me that more weight had been forward on the foot, as it would have been if the bird were ducking its head and then swiveling it to look up.

I had learned what track is made by that gesture the only way it can be learned, by watching a similar bird do a similar thing on the ground and then going over to see what the track looked like. By doing this time after time with bird after bird, animal after animal, person after person, I became a tracker.

Since I began tracking at the age of eight, I have never seen a track being made without wanting to go over and examine it. With each track I add a little information to what I have been able to gather so far. Bit by bit, I learn to track more completely the mystery at the end of every track.

The tracks painted in the living picture of a bird, a picture indistinct at first but clearer with every track, until I could see the small, sleek, gray head swiveling, swiveling as he picked up the seed and looked for cats, dogs, children, cars, birds after his prize, and bigger, hungrier things looking for an easy meal. His tracks hopped forward and I could see, as I crouched, the brushings of his wings in the snow as he took off. He was gone from the ground, but I could still see him in my mind, darting through the air. I looked in a straight line for the most prominent tree and walked toward it.

Juncoes do not waste time cruising for bugs or soaring around sightseeing. They live the pragmatic life of the straight line. They go right down into the jaws of sudden death, down onto the ground, and live by their wits and their prudence. Birds are a delicacy on almost every predator's menu, and when the Junco lands, he hops around watching and watching, pecking and dropping half of what he pecks at because his head comes back up so fast to see what's after him next.

I brushed the pecked and dropped seeds aside. With a mouthful, he had gone flapping off toward the tree, and when I got to it, there were seeds at the foot of the tree that were like the ones where he had taken off. There was a fresh dust of snow around the seeds and beneath some of them, where he had knocked snow down off the branch as he landed.

He must have felt safe sitting there ten feet above half the things that would like to eat him. He must have known that he was hard to see in the trees and that the hawks would rather take him flying anyway. A fleeing animal is a vulnerable animal, and every carnivore in the forest likes an easy kill.

When he changed the position of the seeds in his gullet, he dropped some of them down over the snow that had fallen from the branch. There were hop marks where he had come down to get the dropped seeds later, but the fact that there was a fine dusting of snow on some of the seeds indicated that he had probably come to that branch before to swallow what he had grabbed from the ground.

There were other hop marks under the snow dust when I blew it away, and they seemed to have the same jittery prudence that the other tracks had had. Of course, I knew the bird, I had seen it around my own feeder. Every species has its specific behaviors, but every individual performs them differently. They're as unalike as people.

I recognized the jittery little tremors, the half steps thought about but left untaken. I had gone out and examined his other tracks after I had watched him one day from my window. I could see him pecking and ducking in that jittery, cocky style of feeding that was as individual as a human gait. I checked how the lighter dust of snow from his takeoff had scattered behind him. I checked where it had fallen in relation to the other fall, and I guessed that either the wind had been drifting in that direction or the bird had taken off in the opposite direction sending the branch back and down as it left and dusting the snow further out than the first fall.

Since it was all I had to go on, I went as I had been taught from the track to the trail, looking far ahead to see where it might be going. I could read the identity from the individual print, but I needed the context in which the trail occurred to make sense of it entirely. The bird was feeding, the branch fall indicated he had flown in the direction of my house, and when I walked back there, I found that same jittery Junco near my own feeder. I sat down to watch him pecking-watching-pecking-watchingpeckingwatching-pecking-watching, until someone finally came out of the house and asked me where the milk was.

• • •

I was fascinated with nature even before Stalking Wolf taught me to track, but my nature-watching was limited by the necessity of sitting and waiting for a long time in a place where we hoped something might happen. Stalking Wolf gave me the tools to track the mystery to its source. He taught me how to teach myself. I have been using the tools he gave me ever since.

Stalking Wolf was an Apache tracker. He had come to New Jersey to be near his son who was stationed there. His grandson, Rick, was my best friend, and Stalking Wolf taught both of us how we could teach ourselves to track, to stalk, to live in the woods, and to survive there. He gave us the questions that would lead us to our answers, but he never told us an answer. He taught me to see and to hear, to walk and to remain silent; he taught me how to be patient and resourceful, how to know and how to understand. He taught me to see invisible things from the trail that all action leaves around itself. He taught me how to teach myself the mystery of the track.

Since Stalking Wolf began teaching me, I have worked every day of my life at learning more and more about nature and about tracking. What I have learned was not easily learned, but anyone willing to take the time could do it. Most of the fundamental principles of how to track are in this book and anyone can learn them. Anyone willing to spend twenty years working diligently at it can learn the minute nuances of it as well. Stalking Wolf thought I had a gift for tracking. Anyone with a greater gift could probably learn the nuances in less time. After twenty years, I am still finding things in tracks that I have never seen before, and I do not believe I am in any danger of running out of discoveries.

School taught me how to read. Stalking Wolf taught me how to learn. I have been learning something every minute since, and there is no better way to unravel the mystery than to watch it move. But mysteries are by nature shy and secretive, and most often, the closest you get to them is the traces left behind by movement and the disturbances left by action. I could not see the bird, but I could see the actions of the bird in the traces he left and in the disturbances made by his actions. I could see what was out of place since he had come and gone, the seeds where they did not grow, the tracks in the snow, the snow itself dusted down where it would not have been naturally. I could see the bird go through his routine almost as surely as if I had stood there watching him.

But a track is a temporary thing. Unless the mud goes suddenly hard and turns gradually to stone, tracks do not last. They fade, and as they dry, the wind sweeps them relentlessly level to ease its way across the ground. Tracks exist at the interface where the sky drags along the surface of the earth. They exist for a relatively brief time in a narrow level near the surface of the ground where the wind and the weather move across, changing the temperature and building information into the track. Wind pushes the tracks flat; rain tries to wash them away. Nature conspires to steal even the traces of passage. Most tracks made in the world go under unseen. I try to follow every one I can.

Each trail is one of a kind. The same combination of weather, land, temperature, and creature are probably duplicated no more often than snowflakes. The same interactions between so many variables probably never recur. Even within the easily identified, habitual gait of a person there are nuances made by the changing flux of emotions as he or she moved. The sheer variety of tracks is astounding; the amount that can be learned from them is irresistible.

Either by gift or by curse, I have a compulsion to know more about nature. I can never get enough. Everything I learn makes me see how much more there is to know and how little time there is in a lifetime to learn it all. Stalking Wolf gave me the tools I needed to pursue my curiosity, and I have been sharpening those tools ever since.

The vision of the world given me by Stalking Wolf has become a window into time. The more tracks I see, the clearer the picture of the animal becomes until I can see him moving as he moved a minute, an hour, a month before I came along. When the tracks stop, I can still see the animal, how it paused, how it rested its body, where it put its paws. The animal is there before me almost real enough to touch, fixed in time by the impression of its track. I see from the track the motion of his feet, the motion of his body; I see the animal itself laying down the mystery of its coming and going.

Nothing makes this picture more vivid to me than a skull. When Rick and I found a skull, it kept us busy for days. We cleaned it, assembled it, drew it, and sketched the animal in around it. When we found a complete skeleton, scattered as it often was over hundreds of yards by the wild dogs, we were busy for weeks. Short of the animal itself making the tracks, nothing pleased us more than a skull.

A skull is the ultimate track a creature leaves. When everything else has been unshaped by time, when every scratch and print is gone, the skull remains. When I find a skull, it's as if I am standing within touch of the second greatest mystery in the universe, the mystery of where creatures go when they leave this greatest mystery of all, the pattern of life living itself, the visible design of the invisible that we call Nature.

The place where you lose the trail is not necessarily the place where it ends. A lost trail always extends beyond the evidence, and even the trails we find are only fragments of the trails that lie beyond our comprehension. When the bird left my feeder and flew, I could trail him only by inference, but his trail went on after I lost it, and I believe it goes beyond the skull as well, although I have no idea what it is like or how to follow it. Skulls simply mark the point of departure and the direction of flight, like the brush of a bird's wing in the snow.

I found my first skull in a swamp a mile or so from my house in Beachwood, right off the Toms River, in a place that is a marina and a parking lot now. It was only a pile of broken bones when I found it, but I took it home and fit the pieces together until I had the answer to what it was.

But every answer brings with it the inevitable question: *What has this thing got to do with everything else?* There is only one answer to that question but you have to find it out for yourself a little at a time over a lot of years. The question of what the bones made led me to the question of what kind of skull it was, and the answer to that question led to the question of how the animal had lived and where he fitted into the larger pattern of life.

I am still following the trail of questions that I picked up when I made that little pile of bones into a skull. This book is the story of that trail as I have come down it so far. It begins when I was seven. The pine trees came all the way down to the river then. The houses in even the most settled part of the Pine Barrens were few and far between. Outside Toms River they were scattered in little clumps or strung out at erratic intervals along roads made of hardpacked sand and gravel. There were not enough people in the entire Pine Barrens to make a decent size city. From Asbury Park to Trenton, from Camden to Cape May, larger than Grand Canyon National Park, stretched a wilderness of pitch pine and underbrush cut by an endless tangle of sand roads without names or numbers.

Along the roads, a few hundred native Pineys went back and forth between villages like Hog Wallow and New Egypt in old cars and trucks dying slowly from the assaults of foot-high bumps and axle-deep potholes. But they rarely got out of their cars. A hundred yards off any sand road, there is probably still a place where no human being has stood in a century.

But it's dangerous to go and look. The road sinks half a foot below the brush that packs the space between thirty foot pines, and a traveler who goes ten yards into the woods cannot look back and find the road again. About twice a year someone wanders into the Pine Barrens and dies trying to find their way out. Even the Pineys, whose families have lived in the Pine Barrens for more generations than any of them can remember, stick to the roads.

I always went *across* the roads, following deer runs,

making my own trails, running down any track I found. I have loved the woods as long as I can remember, and I have lived in them all my life. We lived in the fringes of the forest, just off the river, but my back door opened onto the wilderness. To me it was only my back yard. If my parents asked me where I was going, I always told them, "Just camping in the back yard." I meant it and it was true. But to me that back yard fanned out for hundreds and hundreds of square miles. I had to wander the Grand Tetons and go to California before I found the back fence.

I rarely told my parents what went on in the woods, and much of this book will probably come as a surprise to them; but I knew how much they worried about me, and I was afraid that any adventure I told them about might have frightened them into keeping me closer to home. Some of the things that happened to me would certainly have cost me my freedom if I had mentioned them, so I said nothing. The woods were my life and still are. I could not risk losing them. There were trails to follow there, and mysteries to be tracked down. Some callings cannot be ignored.

At first, I had only my curiosity and my *Golden Book of Nature* to guide me, but all that changed one day when I was walking along the river a short way down from my house. I was walking along the bank looking for fossils when I ran into a small but muscular, dark-haired boy doing the same thing. As far as I knew, I was the only one in New Jersey who had even the least interest in fossils or knew enough to go along the river bank looking for them.

I asked him what he was doing, and he said, "Looking for fossils." My heart started pounding. Finally, I had somebody to talk to! Somebody who could understand what I was saying and cared about it. We sat down on a log at the edge of the river around eight o'clock in the morning and began to talk about nature. By noon, we were colleagues, by three we were friends. Eventually, we were to become brothers.

There were places where our skills and knowledge overlapped, but more often than not, they complemented each other. Rick, small, muscular, slim, was a better runner and a better stalker than I was. He had a knack for stalking, and he moved far more quietly than I did, even allowing for the difference in size. But I had a passion for tracking, and I was better at that. There was rarely any competition between us, and we were inseparable during the whole period of my training by his grandfather.

After we had talked through half the afternoon, Rick took me home with him to meet the man who would be my teacher and guide for the next nine years. I was in awe of Stalking Wolf from the beginning. He was of medium height and lean, like his grandson Rick, but his features were classically Indian. There were centuries of dead civilization in his face, and his eyes seemed to be looking at things very far away that distracted him. He seemed to be watching some complex totality that absorbed most of his attention.

It was years before I realized how far his perceptions extended, how much he saw in a glance, how much he heard, how incredibly much he *knew*. But it was clear from the instant I first met him that he knew more of what was worth knowing than anyone I would ever meet. Rick idolized him, and the longer I knew Stalking Wolf, the more I understood why.

Stalking Wolf was very old, and he drifted into reveries that made him seem as if he might be senile when I first met him. But I realized later, when I had seen with amazement how keen his senses were, that he had simply gone inside of himself for a moment to check his perceptions against the pattern of the world. Only after he had taught me how to be silent did I realize that he was stopping his own motion so he could tell the disturbances around him from his own.

It is a silence out of which the tracker listens for the scolding of birds deeper in the woods, or the sound that crackles the branches against the rustle of the wind. Only by silence and rapt attention can anyone hope to feel the ripples in the flow of life in the woods, which spread outward from an intrusion or a disturbance. The scolding of a jay will put every bird within earshot on edge.

Birds are the lookouts of the woods; they spread local alarms. You can hear their cries going back and forth through the air like emergency calls. A man going through the woods churns up as much noise as he churns up landscape. All you have to do to hear it is be quiet and listen. Stalking Wolf's silences were the mark of his skill, the habit of a long practiced art. He was the grandson of a medicine man, and a tracker and hunter for his tribe. To Rick and me, he was the Spirit of the Woods. I believe that he trained us the way he himself had been trained as a child in the last years of the nineteenth century. He taught us a way of life which Rick and I tried to live by.

He was like an uncle who helps with the training of his brother's sons, aloof but affectionate, judgmental but secretly amused, gentle and harsh, guiding without directing. What he taught us permeated everything we did. He taught us to look for subtleties, for nuances, and we had to be quick to catch his hints.

I asked him once why he was so still at times, and he said, "To see better." I may have looked puzzled, but I didn't say anything because neither Rick nor I wanted Stalking Wolf to think we were stupid. Besides, we knew he would never give us the answer to anything directly. Usually, we said we understood and then went away and figured it out between ourselves. Then we went back to Stalking Wolf and told him what we had done and what had been the results. Stalking Wolf would either give us his approval of what we had done or he would tell us we hadn't looked, or hadn't been as quiet as we thought we had.

Then he would give us a hint about what we should do to do whatever we did better, until we finally figured out a way that was workable for us. Without his guidance, we might have learned part of what we did learn, but it would have taken us ten times as long, and some of it we would never have gotten at all. He gave us information that would lead us on to the next step a bit at a time, and he always waited until we had incorporated what we had learned before he nudged us toward something else.

Stalking Wolf led us out of childhood into a unique kind of manhood. We came to our skills as he had come to his, through a series of ideas and understandings that could only be gotten out of experience. He taught us to make use of everything, to live with the least disruption of the earth, to revere what we took from the woods, to master our fear, to hone our special skills sharper and sharper, to expand our senses and our awareness, to live in the space of the moment and to understand eternity.

I learned from Stalking Wolf a skill that could encompass everything I met. I learned to track, not animals or men, but disturbances, things knocked out of place, minute and indistinct traces, the ghost of a print, a stone turned wrong side up, a fragment of hair on a branch.

Stalking Wolf taught us how to be silent and watch what was going on. He had a special look that said he was giving us a hint to something that would seem obvious to us in a moment. When he saw that I didn't understand why he had to be silent to see better, he said, "Go feed the birds."

Rick and I immediately got some seed and went outside to feed the birds. Stalking Wolf came out and watched us and giggled into his hand. He looked away whenever we looked back to him for approval. We tossed the seed. We laid it down. We put it in piles. Nothing pleased him. Finally, he shook his head and went in.

Every time he saw me after that, he would ask me if I had learned to feed the birds yet. I said I didn't know how he wanted me to feed them. And he said, "How would you give food to me?"

He looked like he was going to burst out laughing at any instant, and I nodded and went away to look for Rick. When I found him I said, "How would you give food to your grandfather?" Rick was used to questions like that and he did not look at me as if I was crazy as someone else would have. We could not afford the luxury of being afraid to sound foolish. We burned for answers, and we asked whatever questions came to mind without reservation. Neither of us ever laughed at the other for asking. "I'd hand it to him" he said finally.

I was afraid he was going to say that. "He wants us to hand the food to the birds, as if they're our friends." Rick said that maybe if we put some seed in our hands and sat very still, the birds might come down and take it. I reminded him that these were not park birds but wild ones, but Rick said that if Stalking Wolf wanted us to do it, it was probably no more impossible than all the other things we thought we could never do or understand.

It seemed like a good way to start anyway. We lay on the lawn with the seed in the palm of our hands and stayed as nearly motionless as we could all afternoon. A few birds came close to the ground while we were there, but none ever came within arm's reach. Toward dark, we gave up and came in. I shrugged at Stalking Wolf and said I guessed we weren't still enough. Stalking Wolf shook his head as if we were very foolish. "When should you feed your friends?" he said.

It took me a minute to realize what he meant, but the next morning long before dawn, Rick and I were lying in the dew-wet grass with our hands extended and our palms full of birdseed. We had perfected some measure of stillness from watching things in the woods, but this required not moving for hours, and it would have been far harder if we hadn't been as intent on it as we were.

The thought of feeding the birds like our brothers was a vision worth believing in. It made anything possible. In the middle of false dawn, the birds came awake and blasted the morning warning all over the woods. And in a while, a house sparrow swooped down and took a flying peck. Perhaps an hour of swooping passes later, one landed and pecked some seed from my hand. I could feel the tiny pinprick of its spurs digging into my finger. Then he cocked his head sidewards up my arm and looked directly into my eye. He blinked, shook a little bit, and took off again as if he was pretending that he hadn't seen me until he got out of reach.

They had been eating out of Rick's hand for ten

minutes. He was always more still than I was, but I could usually stay still longer. Some creatures approach according to how still you are, while others approach on the basis of how long you've been still. We learned to stalk what we tracked. We learned to survive in the woods problem by problem, until we could go alone into the woods with nothing but a knife and still survive.

More important, we learned a world view in which Nature is a being larger than the sum of all creatures, and can be seen best in the flow of its interactions. In the movement of each animal, all animals move. I am not sure if these were Stalking Wolf's own ideas or the ideas of his tribe, but Rick and I took them as articles of faith to live by, and we devoted our lives to living in the woods as much as we could and learning everything that was there. We spent most of the next nine years doing exactly that.

We lived on a mixture of what Stalking Wolf had told us and personal conjecture, which we believed to be the True Indian Way of Life. We worked toward this ideal in everything we did. Indian braves were always fit. We rowed, a heavy rowboat, against the tide in the Toms River and cut wood every day. Indian braves were trained as warriors. We took Kung Fu with a neighbor and practiced our kicks continually in front of the cabin we built in the Pines. The life we led kept us fit. Walking, running, crawling all day long, or sitting motionless as a tree for hours at a time waiting to see something miraculous toned us better than any planned system of exercises could have. And we tracked constantly once Stalking Wolf showed us how to learn the secrets. Before that, we watched.

We watched *Everything*: animals, birds, plants, insects, weather, sunlight, stars, fossils, people, hundreds of things. We watched the animals at first. We sat in swamps, in the woods, near lakes, by streams, along the river bank, any place an animal might live. And we waited. And waited. When we were lucky, we saw something special. When we didn't, we saw something else.

And then we learned about tracking. We tracked

everything that moved and some things that didn't. We tracked ourselves. We tracked other people. We tracked animals, cars, snails. We no longer had to wait for nature to come to us. Before we learned to track, our wandering had been guided only by the range of our memory. We went places we were familiar with. But once we could track, we could always backtrack ourselves if we got lost, and year by year our range increased.

From my literal back yard, we went deeper and deeper into the woods until, by the time we were sixteen, there was not a place in the Pine Barrens where I could be lost. We stayed away for longer and longer periods of time as our parents got used to our spending every spare moment studying nature. We kept up our schoolwork for the most part, and we stayed out of trouble, except for being continually late and forever out of reach. We were, if you don't count lies of necessity, model boys for that time and place.

Our tracking began when we were still eight. We found a huge paw print with claws in the mud a mile or so up from Rick's house, and we dragged Stalking Wolf down to see it, jabbering at him all the way down about it being the print of the Jersey Devil because it had claws and it was so huge.

The folklore of our childhood had been full of tales of the Jersey Devil. I always liked to talk to the old Pineys who had lived in the woods so long that there was no recollection in the family of having lived anywhere else. They had incredible stories about the huge, hairy creature that robbed graves and tore people limb from limb. The Jersey Devil was a real creature to me then, and I loved stories about him though I lived in absolute terror of ever running into him. One day I would meet the Jersey Devil face to face in a way I couldn't even conceive of when we dragged Stalking Wolf out to look at the track.

Stalking Wolf looked at the print and then went up a little way and looked some more. He stood looking around a while before he went over to some bushes near one of the tracks and peered in. Then he came back. We waited breathlessly for confirmation that we had indeed discovered an authentic print of the Jersey Devil.

Stalking Wolf shook his head and said that it was a brown and white male dog about 65 pounds who was very excited because he had picked up the scent of the rabbits or the racoon. He told us about ten other things about the dog and then he told us everything it had done while around the swamp. Rick and I were beside ourselves shouting, "What rabbits?! What racoon?!" Exuberance was our one flaw as nature watchers. We would see one wondrous thing, and we would jump around celebrating it and chasing away the fifty other fantastic things we could have seen.

Stalking Wolf showed us the rabbit tracks and told us where the rabbit had gone and come back from and why. He showed us where the dog had picked up the scent and how his gait had changed. The tracks went up to the bush and then leapt away where the rabbit had scurried out of the swamp grass. He pointed out where the rabbit had run, drawing the dog away from where we were. He showed us where she had lost him finally, and where the dog had gone up the hill grumbling and following his nose.

Then he took us back to where we started and showed us the nest and the baby rabbits the mother had been distracting the dog from. We were astounded. "How did you know all that?" we kept asking him. Finally he told us about the tracks and showed us how to read them. We couldn't hear enough of whatever he wanted to tell us about it. At first he drew tracks for us, but then he made us draw them ourselves. Next, we went out and looked for tracks and drew them using different kinds of shading to give depth. When we could draw a track exactly, we started to draw partial tracks until we could tell them apart from only one or two faint lines.

With every track, Stalking Wolf would tell us about the animal that made it, the family it belonged to, and why its track was the way it was. Why the Indians walked like the fox with one foot in front of the other in a straight line. Why the groundhog with its broad chest could never make the in-line tracks of a fox. This did not occur overnight, but over months and often years. Tracking became a preoccupation with us. We tracked everywhere we went. Whenever we watched anything, we always went back later and looked at its tracks to match them up and what we had seen the animal do.

Rick liked to track, and he was a good tracker, but tracking came to me with amazing ease. I worked at it, but it was always a joy to do. I never tired of it. Rick was into stalking and watching nature more than tracks themselves. I wanted to be able to do what Stalking Wolf had done, to be able to look at the tracks and recreate what happened as surely as if I was looking back in time.

It took a long time of constant effort to learn to do that. We tracked everywhere. On the two-lane macadam road that was the biggest highway short of the Parkway, there was a butcher store where the owner smoked his own meat. Rick and I used to go there and learn his techniques after we got involved in taxidermy, but we liked this place especially because it had a bare spot of soft ground near the doorway that never completely dried out. The sets of tracks put down there were endless.

We would sit off to the side and watch someone walk in, and then we would rush over and follow his tracks marking where he stopped or turned or tied his shoes. We would draw the print and mark it with comments like, "Limp from hurt foot, two weeks later," and "Fat men toe out."

When we had fixed the track and the person in our minds, we would smooth out the dirt and wait for the next person to come along. When a woman went storming in with a complaint and came back out mollified, the difference in her tracks was obvious when we ran over to look. The long wedging plumes of dirt in front of the pointed toes going in and the firm even stride with clearly defined prints coming back out could not have contrasted more.

It took us years before we could do it with great precision, but we were improving and we were weaving everything we learned into everything else we did. When we watched the animals, we went over and tracked what we had just watched. When we walked back along our own trail, we following our incoming tracks and watched how much they had deteriorated. Sometimes we would stop at every change in the steady walking pace of the tracks and go over what we did at that point on the way in and why.

We intentionally made footprints when we came to a new kind of soil and put little sticks in them to measure their deterioration. We checked our past footprints every time we passed them to see what changes the weather and time had brought about in them. We would spend a whole day or so watching a track deteriorate, just putting a footprint in the ground and sitting there watching it dry out and go grain by grain into the oblivion of the wind. Sometimes we put sticks and string around the tracks to keep the animals off them, and watched the way they changed over a period of months.

We did this over a period of years, track by track, in every kind of soil we could find, and in each soil we watched for a change in the tracks associated with every change in weather. When we were waiting for some creature to show itself, getting ourselves into position so we were part of the landscape for a long time before the creature came out of his burrow, we would make a print in the ground with a deer foot we carried with us and watch how it deteriorated over an hour or two.

We put another print down near it every few minutes to see how much difference there was between the two and if they went through the same changes. We did that kind of thing constantly. Wherever we were, if there was nothing else worth watching, we watched the tracks change until we could see some of the minute variations that Stalking Wolf could see.

We learned to track and stalk, we learned to live in the wilderness and then learned to survive in it. We learned, by living, how to live. We became men and brothers in the woods. We came of age in the woods, and we came alive. Old Stalking Wolf guided us. This book is the story of how we did it and how I have applied what Stalking Wolf taught me.

Very little of this book will have to do with the criminal cases in which I have been involved because some of them are still under investigation and others involve details I cannot make public without disturbing the privacy of people who have suffered enough. Criminal tracking challenges almost all of my skills, but there is no joy in it. At the end of a case, no matter what decision is reached, there is doubt and uncertainty, anger and controversy. Much of it can never be resolved, and even those things that are certain have a way of deteriorating like a track in a heavy rain under the arguments of lawyers. The truth, when it comes in words, is always a matter of interpretation.

In this book, I have tried to tell my version of the truth and how I came to it. These words are my tracks, this book is my trail; I am at the end of it somewhere, looking for other tracks and the meaning beyond them.

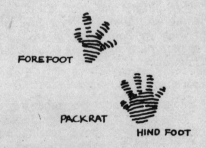

FOREFOOT

PACKRAT

HIND FOOT

MOUSE TRACKS

2/Go and Ask the Mice

It amazes me, when I look back, how little of all that Stalking Wolf taught me was done in words, and how deftly everything was done. He never gave me a direct answer, and when he had something to teach us, he arranged it so that it was something we suddenly needed desperately to know.

He took us tracking one cold December day when the temperature changed, as it does in New Jersey, four or five times from freezing to above freezing in the same day. We made some tracks in the early morning ground and waited and watched as the temperature played havoc with their shape. "That was great!" we told Stalking Wolf when we were finished, but he shrugged a modest disagreement. When he spoke, his hand came up

20

as if it were the true speaker and made pictures to fill in where there were no words.

English is a bad language for certain kinds of words. It hasn't got much for ideas like *wholeness of feeling*. *Nature* is the best word English can come up with to describe something as various yet as indivisible as the bond between all living things. Most of what it feels like to *be there* in the woods is inexpressible in any language. The only language for some things is experience. Some experiences simply do not translate. You have to *go* to *know*.

Stalking Wolf's hand made pictures of experience for which there were no words in either Spanish or English, for concepts thought to be daydreams in New Jersey. There was no way for him to say to us that we should never so focus our attention that we were not also aware of the larger pattern around us.

Where our schools were forcing us to pay total attention, Stalking Wolf was teaching us intermittent attention, a constant refocusing between minute detail and the whole area around it, between the track and the whole pattern of the woods.

When we said what a great experience it had been to sit and watch the track deteriorate, Stalking Wolf said, "The racoon liked it. The squirrel disapproved. The rabbits shook their heads at it, and the deer had no feeling for it at all." His hand moved the animals in to look over our shoulders to see what we were staring at so intently that they could come up on us unnoticed like that. The fingers shrugged and went away again like the animals had while we sat staring at the track.

Rick and I groaned at all we had missed again. "You do not look," Stalking Wolf said as if he were laughing at us.

"But we had to see the track," I said, "You told us to watch the track."

He tried not to laugh. "How do you eat a deer?" he said. His hands made a shape much bigger than his mouth. His eyes did what they always did. They looked at me and then looked away. They came back to my eyes again like a beacon focusing its light in my direction on *every* revolution, but for only part of the time. When he listened he seemed to be listening to a totally different conversation with his other ear. I had thought that that motion was only an idiosyncrasy of the body, a tic from being old perhaps, but it was how he took in all those things that we did not.

"In little pieces," I said. It seemed so obvious looking backward from the answer. It was a long time before I could judge the rate of change in a track or something else I was watching so that I knew just how much time I could spend on each thing and still catch the subtle changes. Stalking Wolf always knew what was going on. If you spoke in a room where he was sleeping, he knew everything that was said.

When he taught us stalking, we had to sneak up on him. But we were never able to do it. He would turn before we got close enough to touch him and tell us exactly how we had come up behind him, where we had brushed against a tree, and where we had stepped on a twig. And he was always right. If we spent three hours sneaking up on him, he was aware of us for at least two of them.

He knew exactly how much of his attention he had to devote to each thing to measure it and to keep the vision of the whole pattern going at the same time so he could see the disturbances. Because he knew the daily pattern of life in the forest, he knew what was normal for the weather and the time of day. He knew how much bird activity there should be, which shift of predators was around, when the mice would be running from place to place. But he had to keep an ongoing record of it in his mind.

He had an incredible memory for detail, as if he took the whole scene in instead of focusing on one part of it as most people do. He could recall every detail because he knew the experience as a whole. Everything fitted in with the ongoing pattern of the weather he kept in his head. I believe he slept with his window open so that the record could be kept even while he was asleep, although

I do not believe that he was totally asleep for very long at any one time.

Maybe he had figured out how much of his brain he could afford to rest at any one time and for how much time he would have to shut it down altogether for recuperation. He always seemed to know what was happening all around him, as if he had ears and eyes all over his body.

Once while we were walking in the woods, Rick was looking around and twisting his head up toward the branches and down onto the path as a way of scanning things. I believe the fact that he moved his head so much instead of moving his eyes had a lot to do with why he was not as good a tracker as he might have been. We went under a tree while Rick was looking up and Stalking Wolf said, "Let it sleep."

He kept walking but we begged him to tell us *what* was sleeping. He nodded at a Great Horned Owl on a branch above our heads. I was sure he had not looked up as we had approached the tree, or as we passed under it, but I gradually came to realize that he did not need to *see* it to know it would be there. He knew the way owls lived; he knew what kind of trees they liked; he had seen the fresh owl pellets on the ground at the base of the tree; he knew when owls flew and when they rested. He knew the activity of small rodents for the time of day and temperature. He could probably have told us what tree the owl would be in if he had stayed at home.

We pleaded with him to tell us how he knew, and he said that the mice had told him. When we wanted to know *what* the mice had told him, he said to go and ask the mice. So Rick and I spent the next couple of weeks studying mice. Thereafter we watched them to see what they were doing at that time of year, and we found that Stalking Wolf was right. Once we knew the pattern of life for the mice, we knew the pattern of life for everything that eats mice, and we could generalize to most other small rodents until we had a chance to study them the same way.

We also knew to some extent the lives of the things-

that-ate-the-things-that-ate-the-mice. Stalking Wolf did
not simply tell us where the mice were or why they were
there. He let us go and discover the whole thing for ourselves. We learned whatever we made important in our
lives. The mice were good medicine. They led us beyond
their mystery to the mystery of the way the lives of the
animals were interdependent. They led us to an idea of
how the whole fabric meshes together, although it may
be that you have to live as long as Stalking Wolf and observe as keenly as he did before the pattern makes total
sense.

When you can see that pattern, you can see the spirit-
that-moves-through-all-things instead of merely catching isolated flashes of its motion in good medicine and
omens. An omen is an insight that changes your way of
seeing the world. It is a landmark against which everything that follows or preceded it comes to be measured.
An omen is the shadow of the spirit-that-moves-in-all-
things. I believe that Stalking Wolf could perceive that
spirit directly, and that that was what he was watching
and listening to when he seemed so far away.

The more we learned to let our attention wander and
come to rest on the thing at hand just often enough to
catch the disturbances, the better we became as trackers
and as observers of the woods.

But I had a strong tendency to zero in on things, to
blot out everything else and just concentrate all my attention on the track. I would be aware of everything as
long as I was stalking, but when I got to an interesting
trail, I went track by track with my head down like a
bloodhound smelling along the ground.

I found the trail of a huge deer that way once, the
kind of deer it would have been good medicine just
to see. He walked down one of the trails about twenty
yards and then leaped up into the bushes and went down
several branches of the same run. I followed it step by
step, crouching down half the time, and before long, I
was back out on the road coming up behind my own
tracks.

Even before I looked I knew those deer tracks were

going to be in all my footprints. I was mortified. The deer had been stalking *me*! That was bad enough, but Stalking Wolf was going to be out with us for the weekend, and in a few hours he was sure to come by that place and laugh at those tracks until he cried.

I decided that the best thing was to tell him. So I did, and he limited himself to a half smile and said, "Wait." His hand made a space of time it was hard to misunderstand. "Follow," he said. Then he went down the road leaving fine, clear, obvious footprints for me to follow. It was so obvious that I thought there must be some nuance of the track that should tell me if I was being circled, so I scrutinized each track as I went, looking for something I didn't know to look for before.

The track went around the bend and then up a trail to the left. I went up it step by step, looking for I did not know what. The tracks got a little funny, though I could not say how, and then they just stopped. I stood up and looked down the blank trail. I felt something behind me and looked over my shoulder, but Stalking Wolf ducked away around to the front of me in his crouch and I didn't *see* him. He could get right up next to a person and stay out of their sight. Rick and I practiced matching strides with people in the house and walking directly in their footprints as their foot left them, then dropping off and slipping away unnoticed. We tripped a few heels learning, but we did our early practicing on each other, and no one noticed.

Stalking Wolf had been walking in my footsteps half way down the trail. Finally he burst out laughing. I couldn't believe he was there. "How did you do that?" I wanted to know. I had to wait until he stopped laughing to get an answer. He walked backward down the trail without looking and when he got to the road, there were only the footsteps he had walked up it in. He had put his feet, going backward and without looking, into exactly the places he had put his feet in coming up. Rick eventually learned to do it very well, but it was always beyond me; at least, the exact register Stalking Wolf had.

"But where were you?" I demanded. He hopped off the trail and stood beside it leaning against a tree. It felt worse than having been trailed by the deer. "How could I have missed you?" I wanted to know. I thought he had some secret way to make himself invisible that we did not know about yet.

"I don't think you look," he said. And I realized he was right, I hadn't looked. I had been so intent on the track that I had not kept checking it against the pattern of the woods.

There was no need for a lecture or an explanation. From then on, I looked less at the tracks. Once I had registered what I could of things that would not change for a while, like size and species, I looked not for the track, but for where the track was going. When I lost a track after that, I would scan ahead to see where it was going. When I looked in the intervening spaces where a paw or a foot should have come down, I usually found the minute scratch and scuff marks where the prints should have been.

Very early in our training, we had drawn the track and then learned to identify the animal from it from smaller and smaller portions of the track. After we learned to look ahead and around instead of continually down, we tracked more easily and much, much faster.

Stalking Wolf could track at a dead run, and once you learn to track that way, it is not difficult to track from a moving jeep. Stalking Wolf led us to situations where we could learn certain principles, but once he had shown them to us, it was up to us to put in the hours and hours of practice it took to acquire the skill. Stalking Wolf showed us that tracks deteriorate differently under different conditions, but it was up to us to go around putting little sticks in every track we saw to measure how much it had gone down since we last saw it.

He taught us how to learn and we learned. From time to time, he would come out in the woods with us and see how far we had progressed in our skills and give us a hint of new directions to go in. He had been moving us in the direction of survival as well as training us to stalk and to track. He was teaching us to live *with* the woods rather than *in* them.

He always told us that Nature would never hurt us if we acted rightly toward her and did not panic. It became the unshakable foundation on which we based all our actions in tight situations. It was the major tenet of our faith. Fanatics that we were we put our belief to the test continually. But whenever we went with our instincts, we always fared better than when we depended solely on reason. But in ordinary circumstances, when there was no immediate threat, learning and logic had much more to do with our survival.

All day long as we had been watching the weather modify the track, we gave no thought to time. But it began to get late in the day, and Rick and I suddenly realized that we were hungry and had brought nothing with us to eat. It was getting long past when Stalking Wolf would normally have started for home on a day trip, and we kept waiting for him to say it was time for us to start back. But he seemed ready to settle in for the night.

We waited for him to tell us what we should do next, and we got hungrier and hungrier. Finally I said, "Well, Rick, let's go fishing." But the lake was frozen over and we had no tools for ice fishing. Stalking Wolf sat there laughing at us as we ran over to the lake and back. We got back out of breath and told him the lake was frozen over. He nodded as if it were interesting but tangential information. We waited for him to tell us what we were going to eat, and finally Rick asked him what we were having for supper.

The old man said, "Tortuga." Rick shouted "Tortuga! Of course!" and ran back toward the edge of the lake. I ran after him demanding to know what we were running after. "Snapping turtle!" he called back over his shoulder. We had been digging in the frozen mud for fifteen minutes before Stalking Wolf came over with a thin stick about three feet long. He walked along looking at the ground and pushed his stick in. He waited a minute, then pulled it back out, as if he was throwing back a fish that was not perfect. Then he poked the stick in again and waited and threw back another.

On the third try, he put it part way in and it went tap-tap. Rick and I started digging around Stalking Wolf's stick, and only a few feet down, there was a huge snapping turtle still too torpid to move. I was going to ask Stalking Wolf how he did it, but I knew he would only tell me to look, so I looked closely at the other two places where he had put his stick in the mud, and there was a little raised rim of mud where the turtle had dug himself in.

When we had cooked the turtle in its shell with some herbs and had eaten it, it was clear that Stalking Wolf intended for us to spend the night. But we hadn't brought sleeping bags or even the doubled blankets filled with rags that we sometimes used for sleeping bags, and we had no cabin. We asked Stalking Wolf where we were going to sleep and he said to make a lean-to out of pine trees. We had worked our way through enough of the *Boy Scout Manual* to know how to do that, and when it was finished, Stalking Wolf told us to fill it with old, dry pine needles. When we had it filled, we built a fire with a reflector to throw heat into the lean-to. Then we buried ourselves in the needles and went to sleep warmer than I could remember being with my sleeping bag.

After that, whenever Rick and I went out to camp, something was missing, like the matches, or the food, or our knives, until finally we realized that Stalking Wolf was taking those things away from us to force us to survive without them. Eventually we could live in the woods with only our open hands. We knew the berry seasons and where to get edible roots. We knew how to fish and where to find our food. And if we had to, we knew how to snare a rabbit or kill a deer.

Our snares were clumsy attempts that merely detained an animal rather than killed it. Stalking Wolf's snares always looped only the neck, and his sapling lashed aloft like an executioner's cord, snapping their necks instantly. One instant they were running in the full flow of the woods, and the next they were gone. It always gave me something to think about whenever I set a snare.

Stalking Wolf set *one* snare to show us how to make the catchpin slip easily and untie the bent sapling when the rabbit triggered it. He did not kill animals except for food, and then generally only if it was a matter of survival. He had killed the rabbit only to show us how it could be done, for when we really needed it to survive. He had made us go two days hungry waiting for the snare to be tripped when we finally did the snaring ourselves, and we were lucky that the snare had something in it in less than a week. But Stalking Wolf had read the tracks and put his snare down on the rabbit run and had caught a rabbit coming back from wherever he had been. He gave us the rabbit and told us to cook it. After we had struggled, skinned it, cleaned it, and roasted it, we ate it. It did not taste like any rabbit I have ever eaten before or since.

After we had learned to stalk each other, Stalking Wolf had us stalk him. When he thought we had mastered it, he sent us to stalk animals. Every few weeks, he came and watched us and told us where we had made the animal aware of our presence or how we had stepped on a twig instead of looking for it and stepping under it. He showed us how to stalk a deer for hours until you can come up so close that you can reach out and touch him.

If there was a predator around, Stalking Wolf would give the deer a smack on the behind for being so careless, but as often as not, he would stand along the trail and let his hand hang out like a branch. It would drift over the backs of the deer as they went by, and once one of them stopped to scratch itself against his fingers. Stalking Wolf started scratching its back and it rubbed back and forth as if the hand were a branch.

Rick and I got good enough to get within sight of a deer almost immediately, but it was two years before Rick touched his first deer. I had to wait until six months later when they were less skittish because they knew hunting season was over. Rick was always a better stalker and he and Stalking Wolf were very happy for me when I finally did it. No one else believed me, of course, and it was one of the rare times that I mentioned what really went on in the woods.

Stalking Wolf came with us that weekend to celebrate, and after we had eaten, we sat around the campfire and coaxed him into telling us stories. Stalking Wolf was probably one of the last Indian boys to be brought up in the old ways. I believe he put us through the training he had been put through. He told of how the braves of his tribe had stalked their deer in the same way we had. He told us of his good friend Medicine Deer and the true test of stalking, "bear smacking."

Boys of his village often teased one another to do it, and from time to time someone did. Stalking Wolf and Medicine Deer had come upon fresh bear tracks one day. They were fifteen then, young warriors of a defeated people without a battle to offer their courage or their skill a chance to win them distinction. Because they were young, they took whatever risks were available and Medicine Deer claimed the right to stalk the bear since he found the first track. Stalking Wolf's only choice was to watch from a distance. To have gotten closer would have infringed on Medicine Deer's daring.

Medicine Deer went forward, moving with the rustle of the leaves on feet turned softly inward, going in bursts of small well-placed steps like any creature whose life depends on not being seen. He moved from tree to tree in a low, fast-moving semicrouch. He froze when the wind stopped rustling the leaves. The bear nibbled berries from a bush oblivious. Medicine Deer moved the last few feet in short, quick steps.

When he stood behind the bear, he did not smack it right away. The measure of his courage was in how long he stayed risking each second that the bear would catch his scent on a sudden change of the wind and turn on him at close quarters. Finally, he gave a warhoop and smacked its tail. The bear gave a howl of bewilderment and indignation before it turned to pursue him. Medicine Deer was a great runner, and he was outrunning the bear, giving loud warhoops of victory, when he stumbled and broke stride. The bear caught and killed him.

I asked Stalking Wolf if he had ever smacked a bear, and he said that he had but not since Medicine Deer. Some things, he said, were for young men, and watching the bear kill Medicine Deer had made him very old. I could not understand that then, and although there were few if any bears in the Pine Barrens, I swore to myself that if I ever came to a place where there were bears, I would try what Medicine Deer had tried. But my skill was not up to it for a long time, and my luck was not up to it when I finally got my chance in the Grand Tetons.

BLACK BEAR

3/Good Medicine Cabin

By the time I was 10½ or 11, we had moved our campsite so far out into the "back yard" that although we were only five miles as the crow flies from home, nobody except Stalking Wolf would voluntarily walk the distance, especially after dark. We went away for days at a time, telling my parents we would check in at Rick's every day for food and telling Rick's parents we would check in every day at my house. Our parents got together once when we were a day late because we lost count, and we were in big trouble for a month or more.

It was so easy to lose all track of time in the woods; there was so much to see, and the time went by so quickly that often I was certain as I could be that it was a day or two earlier than it was. When Rick did not come out with me, I often had to count the incidents of the stay to figure out what day it had to be.

There were so many fascinating things to be studied and identified. Rick and I had been driving the woman at the storefront library in Beachwood crazy for almost two years, dragging specimens in to compare with the big reference books. The insect books were outstanding, but we didn't make the librarian any happier by bringing our insect specimens in live and letting them crawl around on the color plates until they matched something. I think that woman lived in mortal terror that we would leave behind something poisonous or contagious.

Still, we exhausted every resource before we bothered Stalking Wolf with a problem of identification. He had his own names for things and stories to go with each animal, but we tried not to bother him much, and we resorted to books most of the time for problems of simple identification. We reserved Stalking Wolf for all the points of tracking that couldn't be found in books, and there were plenty of those.

Eventually we got a hardbound sort of atlas of tracks with fifty pages for notes which we filled up in no time. Not long after, I earned some money doing odd jobs and got all the Peterson guides. I started with Roger Tory Peterson's *A Field Guide to the Birds*, which got dog-eared with use in the first week.

We spent a lot of time in the library as well, coming in covered with mud from wading halfway across a swamp to get a flower that we couldn't wait to identify. When we came in straight from school with drawings of something to be identified, we were welcome enough, but the skulls we brought in to look up made us no more popular than the bugs and the mud.

We were always taking specimens. I carried my lab kit with me everywhere. A three inch magnifying glass, a test tube for samples, tweezers, and my knife. We took specimens like a landing party from Venus. Everything interested us. We did not walk from home to the camp-site without learning a dozen new things every time.

The times Stalking Wolf came for a walk with us or camped out with us were major holidays. If Stalking Wolf said, "I'm coming camping with you on Friday," we would be out at the campsite all week cleaning up everything that might look the least bit like litter. Living on the land without blemishing it was something that Stalking Wolf stressed constantly.

I learned more in one day with Stalking Wolf than I learned in any class during a whole year. We went with him everywhere. If he went into the bushes to relieve himself, we went with him for fear of missing something he might say. Every minute we were around him, we were soaking up information that we could use for the rest of our lives. We were going to grow up to be famous naturalists and marry and live with our wives on adjoining ranches in the wilderness then.

The campsite that Stalking Wolf came to most often was what we called the Good Medicine Cabin. Stalking Wolf never defined what good medicine was outside of its obvious meaning of being something beneficial and remarkable, but from the things he identified as good medicine and from what he said about them, I believe that good medicine is any experience so memorable that it just *has* to be a gift from the spirit-that-moves-through-all-things.

Good medicine was a sign that nature was showing you favor by allowing you to be part of some remarkable event or experience. Good medicine could come at any time and came in varying degrees. Some days would be full of interest, but without a startling event. To be good medicine as opposed to the ordinary beauty of the world, a thing had to be so unique an experience that no one who had gone through it could help but comment on it. Good medicine was almost always an event so remarkable that only the setting in which it occurred can be accurately described.

Good medicine announced its presence in marvelous sights, wondrous happenings. Good medicine was also any mystery, no matter how small, whose solution opened to larger, more wondrous mysteries. Bad medicine was a sign of disfavor for the spirit-that-moves-through-all-things. Good medicine came when we were totally engrossed in experiencing nature. Bad medicine came when we were still marching around in our city personalities, or when we were out of our proper sphere of actions.

The Good Medicine Grounds was shown to us by an eagle. Just beyond it, there was a pine tree that had been mauled by lightning and termites until it had only half a trunk and one limb. The tree itself would have been sufficient good medicine by virtue of the way it stood, like it had been beaten but not defeated. I loved that tree the first time I saw it. It was blasted and gnawed, and there was only half of it left, but what there was of it stood straight up and down like a defiant gesture.

We were sitting under it trying to decide where we should build the cabin we had been thinking about, when we heard an enormous flapping of wings. When we looked up, there with the sun behind it, on the last withered branch, was an eagle. It sat there for a while and then it flew away again, but I can still see it in my mind's eye. It was a huge bird, and it had a presence that was more than fifty pounds of feathers should have had.

We watched it with open mouths as it flew away. I expected it to grab the sun in one crooked talon and snatch it away as it flew. We stood numb with the spectacle of the eagle's flight. When that tree finally fell down, giving up to disease what lightning could not take from it, Rick and I carried branches of it home to put in our rooms. Even Stalking Wolf agreed that it was very good medicine indeed, although it would have been better if the eagle had dropped us a feather or two. We had no doubts after that about where to build the cabin.

We built it with painstaking care but very little in the way of tools. We had an old saw that was too dull to be of use to anyone else and a sledge hammer. After we found out how to notch the logs, we got a chisel. My father taught us dovetail notching, and we cut and fitted the cedar logs at each end of the walls. The roof sloped toward the back, and we wove cedar saplings from the swamp to form a mat for the roof. Then we covered those with pine boughs and threw dirt up on it to pack up the holes. Eventually, Pine Barrens grass grew on it.

We rimmed the foundation so water wouldn't erode it. We learned a lot of our construction techniques out of the *Boy Scout Manual*, and we worked our way through it by trying everything instead of just reading about it or watching a demonstration of it by some assistant scout leader. We thatched the walls by tying on clumps of grass, like knotting a broom, and looping the knots over the logs of the wall. We wove grass into the roof as well and put a little sandboxlike wall around it to keep the dirt from washing off. By the second winter, it was as warm and waterproof as a house. But it took us forever to build because, whenever we went into the cedar swamp for logs, we would get sidetracked by some plant or water bug or fish. We lost whole days if there was a snake in the water to watch or a heron fishing downstream. Sometimes it took us a full day to get two logs because we stopped to watch a wasp build a nest in the mud along the bank.

When we finally finished it, the cabin was a small sturdy building somewhere between a hut and a fortress. The door was circular with cross logs that fitted down into the hooks inside the doorway to hold it closed. We finished it when I was eleven, and just in time. The day after we finished it, we suffered our first dog attack.

We were sitting outside eating sandwiches made from the meat we had taken a hike to town to get when we saw them. They were still stalking us, and they had gotten in close enough to embarrass us with our lack of observation. It was definitely not a story we could tell Stalking Wolf, if we lived through it. For a moment, it occurred to me that we might not. There were eleven of them spread out around almost three sides of us, except on the side of the cedar swamp.

If we ran into the swamp, they would all converge on us and pull us down where the muck held us back. It seemed that everywhere I turned my head, there was a dog moving silently into position. One had crawled almost to the edge of the clearing. I couldn't believe how big he was—bigger than I was almost. The other dogs were just as fierce looking; mutts, of course, but only the leanest and most vicious survived the rigors of living wild. Most of them had either Doberman or shepherd in them mixed with almost every other type of dog.

They were not big dogs in weight but no part of them was waste. Everything was muscle etching through the skin. When they moved, their muscles looked like iron bars under their fur. The biggest dog lay at the edge of the clearing with his head between his paws as if he did not want to startle us into bolting for the cabin door before he could get there himself.

Very slowly, I felt around the campfire until my fingers touched the end of one of the burning logs. I counted three with Rick and threw it. The dog ducked out of the way while we dove for the doorway. It charged for the door too late and we yanked the door into place and let it drop into its hooks. The other dogs barked furiously and threw themselves up against the walls trying to knock them in. One even climbed up the stack of logs we had onto the roof trying to shake the cabin down. We weren't worried; the cabin was sturdy as a tree. A deer could have run across the roof without hurting it.

The other dogs tore our camp apart and devoured our food, but eventually they decided that we were impregnable and they went off howling like sirens into the woods. I can still feel the cold shiver that went down my back when I realized that it was only a 50–50 chance that we would beat that huge dog to the door. The dogs had been abstractions for the most part deep in the woods.

We had been treed often enough on the incoming trail when we crossed into their territory, but this was the first time they had come into what we considered our territory, and it was unnerving. Once we were into the deep woods, they were just voices off in the distance howling over the edge of the world. Every once in a while, we would stop what we were doing to listen for distance when we heard that bark that says the dog is running on the trail of something and has no intention of giving up the chase. But it was the first time we had ever met them in force so deep in our part of the woods. It was not something I wanted to do again.

The next time they came at night. We were sitting around the campfire when the light picked up their eyes moving in the bushes around the clearing, and we dove for the door again. We won easily the second time, but there was still a flash of terror in seeing those eyes appear in the darkness and knowing they might have been there for a long time before we knew it.

They battered the cabin for a little while, but they seemed to know it was useless, and eventually they went away. I hated those dogs. I had had my horror with one when I was ten. It was dog-days August, choking hot on the dusty road into the woods but cooler in the pines themselves. I was having a great day. The dust was a gold mine of tracks, and I had been in and out of the trees a dozen times coming up the road. I was only beginning to track, but I followed every trail as far as I could even then.

I was sweaty and tired, and it was that dead, hot part of the afternoon when everything sizzles and the tar bubbles on old macadam roads. It was not such a long walk from my house, and it was only a day trip. I was just about to cut in a large circle and start home again by a different route when I saw it.

I knew what it was as soon as I caught the flash of whiteness. A skull!! It blotted everything else in the forest into invisibility. The world focused only on that skull, and as I got close to the narrow path it lay in the middle of, I could see that it was a complete skull, wonderfully intact, a perfect specimen. I leaned down over the bushes into the dog run to pick it up. The dog must have been lying in the run hiding, or maybe he was crawling up on me all the time. I should have noticed when the birds stopped singing that something tense was going on.

It just came so suddenly out of such dead quiet that the snarl sounded like an explosion that hurled the dog in my face. For a long time the sound of a dog would send that face full of teeth flying at me again out of the bushes, and for years afterward I woke up whimpering and sweating out of the vision of those fangs snapping at my face. I could see that face, with its eyes wide and staring, its ears back, and that long narrow mouth taking bites that could have swallowed my face.

He was a big dog, and the weight of him alone knocked me over backwards. He was black with gray on the back and sides, more Doberman than anything else except possibly shepherd. He was huge and it was all stringy muscle from running all the time. He felt so incredibly heavy, and I kept kicking and screaming and punching trying to get the knife out. I held his face back by one ear, but it was a strong dog. It jerked my arm forward once and its fangs caught me, ripping through my upper lip.

I got to my knife somehow, and I kept stabbing at it and kicking at it until it fell dead on top of me. I was covered with blood, and I flung it off me and leaped on it, stabbing and stabbing and stabbing at it as if its teeth were still snapping shut on my face. The utter horror of those teeth coming at me so fast and so unexpectedly had put me into a frenzy, and I knelt screaming and stabbing for a long time, until I finally realized it was dead. I knelt there and shook.

No other medicine was stronger than bad medicine defeated, and I took his back bones and made a necklace out of them that still hangs on the mirror of my jeep to remind me never to be that careless around dogs again. But for a couple years I didn't need the necklace to remind me; I had the nightmares. Sometimes a howl far off in the Pines would trigger one, and I would wake up in my sleeping bag with that snarling face melting away as I came awake.

He was probably crazy with heat and pain from ulcerations where he had scraped himself in the woods and let it go unattended. I must have killed that dog a dozen times in my sleep before he went away and died completely. Even a long time later, that face would come back at me out of nowhere to remind me. That dog had hunted me in dreams for more than a year, and more than once when I bent to reach for something that looked easy, I would fear that face coming up out of nowhere at me with my death in its mouth. When the dogs came to the cabin, I could see that dog in the pack everywhere I looked. No matter what dogs chased us, it was always *that* dog as far as I was concerned.

We were often chased by dogs on our way in to the Good Medicine Cabin. The whole journey was filled with dangers. Some were simple dangers, like the quick mud or the sameness of the terrain that got so many people utterly, hopelessly lost in such short periods of time. Some dangers were more complex, like Blanchard's dogs.

The wild dogs came out of the municipal dump along four long, ribbony oval runs that fanned out from the dump like the blades of a propeller. One of the runs came past the house of a man called Blanchard. Blanchard put meat out for the dogs and one by one lured them into pens and enclosures they couldn't get back out of.

The dogs hung around there, but he had no control over them. It was almost as if he fed them to keep them from overrunning him. I don't believe that he actually set the dogs on us, but he never did anything to call them off either. We had seen him keep the dogs back with a hose near the house, and when they treed us, they could easily have been lured away with a few pieces of meat thrown into the part of the pack that was left behind. He would have had to have been deaf not to have heard us yelling when the dogs treed us time after time.

They were certainly not tame dogs, but taking handouts had weakened either their desperation or their resolve, and they gave up easily once they had run us up a tree. After a few leaps, they would turn around and go back nearer to the house. If we wanted to go two miles out of our way, we could have avoided the dogs. They seemed to have a perimeter that corresponded roughly to Blanchard's property, although the dogs, for the most part, were still wild and were certainly vicious.

We had to pass along the back of Blanchard's property to get by. The dogs did not usually go outside of their territory, but they would attack anything that came near its boundaries as long as Blanchard kept feeding them. It was as though he had hired an army of vandals as mercenaries and then had to keep them happy for fear they might turn on him. Maybe he let them run their aggressions off by chasing us. I don't know how they came to that complex arrangement, but it seemed to work. The dogs chased us off Blanchard's property, but if we skirted it and were down wind the whole time, and if we moved quickly, we could cross the narrow strip of land they considered theirs without incident.

Once we moved outside the circle of their influence, they abandoned the chase with surprising ease, but that didn't keep them from being intent on our pursuit while it lasted. More than once we had to spend a couple of hours in a tree, pelting them with sticks and insults until Blanchard came out to feed them, or until they got tired of barking.

Rick and I were experts at climbing trees. Hooking our arms around the trunk like a safety belt and snapping it up half a body length at a time, we could almost walk up a tree vertically as fast as we could walk across a fallen log. We got plenty of practice, and the thought of the dogs was always with us until we passed Blanchard's.

Sometimes, if not too many broke off from the pack, we stood and fought them. Nobody ever came out to stop us. Maybe he hoped we'd kill them off. If they caught us too far from a tree, we beat them off with sticks. Miles before we got there, we would start looking for sturdy weapons to fight them off with. I always hoped they would be busy on the far side of his house and we could get past unseen.

I thought about the dogs all the way in until we got past them, and I could not think of them without thinking of that other dog. Every time I came into that part of the woods, I paid in fear and anxiety. The dogs seemed the price of our admission to the wonders we found in the woods. But the dogs were not the greatest danger of the mind. The witch frightened us much more.

Her house was farther into the woods than Blanchard's, and we were terrified of her. She may well have been merely an ugly old woman who had conned some local fools into believing that ugliness alone was a mark of power, but to us, she was a witch. If you believe a thing, and act on that belief, then your actions must be judged in terms of that belief. We really believed she was a witch, and it took no less courage to go past her house than it would have if she really had been a witch.

We believed she was a witch and that she, like the dogs, guarded the entrance to the Pine Barrens. She sat hunched in a rocker on her front porch most of the time, poring over a huge book open in her lap. When we went by, she would eye us suspiciously and cover the book as if we were close enough to decipher it. She was always writing in the book or muttering over it.

We always seemed to pass her house after dark when there was a full moon. There were candles moving around inside the house most of the time. Cars came slowly down the dirt road, winding around it with their lights shooting out oddly through the trees. People went into the house with their heads down as if they could hide who they were that way. We wondered what went on in there, but the house itself seemed powerful and dangerous, and approaching it seemed out of the question. It represented a force that ran contrary to the force of the woods.

In the yard, she had wind chimes made from bones that we convinced each other were human bones. There were more than enough stories in our collection about devil worshipers sacrificing children for it to be credible. We constantly challenged each other to go up to the house. We loved to be scared and to act in the face of our fear. We would go into the cedar swamp alone and sit there for as long as we could. Invariably the others would crawl up and make inhuman groans and shrieks that generally drove us out of the dark even when we were sure it was simply a joke. But the witch's house was a magnitude of fear higher than the cedar swamp.

Nevertheless, one night we got up the courage to creep up and look in the window to see what was going on. Rick went first because he was the best stalker, and I came along a very slow and deliberate second. When we looked in through the window, we saw four people holding hands around a table with a candle in the middle of it. The witch had her hair down out of the knot she usually kept it in, and it flowed in a long white mane down past her waist.

The table was covered with black cloth and it had a series of bones on it. I am sure neither Rick nor I made a sound, but the woman's face turned toward us with her eyes closed and she smiled, as if she had seen us through some other sight and thought that for the moment we were beneath her dignity. We did not wait around for her to change her mind.

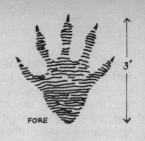

FORE 3"

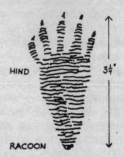

HIND 3½"

RACOON

4/Quick Mud

*The Good Medicine Cabin was built next to a cedar
swamp. A swift running clear-water stream ran out of
the swamp and around the outer perimeter of the
clearing. We knocked over two cedar skeletons and
made a bridge across the stream. While we were
building it, we got the idea for the observation platform.*

Just upstream, we built a platform of logs sticking out
from the bank and straddling the water. We had log
chairs that used the forked tree for a back rest, and we
covered the platform with dirt and had small fires on it.
We even had a railing running around it for a while. It
gave us a perfect view of the swamp and the stream as
well.

We lay on it in summer sunning ourselves in the

44

beams of light that came down through the trees. The patches of sun moved around the platform without pattern and we moved with them, keeping warm in the hot sun. Sometimes we would lie on our stomachs and watch a water snake pulling the string of its own ripples against the current. Sometimes it would lift its head out of the water and curve its chest up so that it looked like a Viking ship under full sail.

Once we watched a racoon in absolute silence until it came and played around the legs of the platform. We wanted it to climb up on the platform with us, but as it began to climb up, we remembered that Stalking Wolf had said that a racoon could rip apart two full-grown German shepherds. Then we wanted it to go away. But it apparently had no grudge against people, and it just investigated us for a little while and went back to its main occupation of survival. We were sorry to see it go.

One late spring day, we lay there following the sun as it climbed over the tops of the cedar trees, warming spots all over the deck at one time. We had just gotten out from swimming, and we were lying there in the splotches of sun to dry off. It was a lazy spring day, and there was a haze over the top of the stream as if the coldness of the stream were making steam against the heat of the air. Everything seemed to slow down as if something of great importance was about to happen.

Before our eyes, like a message from the bottom of the stream, a Green Water Frog rose slowly to the surface. He stopped with just his smirking face and bugged eyes out of the water before he came up onto a stump we had tried to use in the beginning to make the deck. He sat on that for a moment, and then as if he heard something coming, he sprang off it into space. But he never hit the water.

A dark flashing shape darted toward the platform under the water. As the frog sprang, a huge pickerel broke water, caught him in midair, and swallowed him as it fell back into the water again.

It seemed like the most incredible thing we would ever see, and Rick and I went berserk. We jumped up and down and patted each other on the back as if we had planned and executed the whole maneuver. We asked each other over and over again if we saw that and then described it to each other over and over again as if one of us had just come back from somewhere and had missed the whole thing.

The pickerel made a long curve and broke water again as if taking a bow, and we went crazy again, jumping up and down and patting each other on the back until Rick went up against the railing. It broke and he went feet first into the mud. The momentum of his jump put him in up to his arm pits. I looked at him and started to laugh. Rick laughed with me, until he tried to get out and found that he couldn't move. Struggling to reach me and grab a stick I had stretched out to him only worked him in deeper, and although he was not sinking any deeper than his arm pits, there was always the chance that he might slip under without any hope of getting him back out.

The pocket of mud he was stuck in was just inland from the stream. Apparently there was a gully there that water had flowed into from time to time as the stream overflowed its banks. The accumulation of leafmeal and silt had finally filled the depression with a permanent black mud.

Rick wriggled for a while and said he felt bottom, so he was not going to sink any further. But he was stuck and there was no question about it. The suction was holding him like a cork in a bottle, and I could hear it sucking at his legs every time he moved. The mud squished like a hungry mouth when he tried to squirm toward the surface a little more.

I tried for an hour to free him, but it was no use. I even used a rope made of bullbriars to pull him out with, but he was too firmly stuck. We tried everything, including having him reach down and undo his pants so he could slip out of them and break the suction that way. But he could not move his legs to get them out of the pants, and he could not unzip them anyway.

The sun was going down and I was getting worried.

Rick had sunk another couple of inches with all the squirming around, and I was not sure what would happen if he fell asleep, and I did not dare leave him alone to go for help. I did not tell Rick, but there was just as good a chance that what he was standing on was not the bottom but a log, and that if he slipped off it, he would go in over his head without hope of getting back out.

I tried digging him out, but the more mud I pulled back away from him, the closer it drained against his thigh underneath the mud I held back. "We have to break the suction," Rick kept saying. Eventually, it triggered something I had heard once before when a boy had gotten himself stuck in the swamp down the road from Rick's house. He was wedged in the same way as Rick, and the fire department had worked for three hours to pull him out before someone had said, "Just break the suction and he'll come right out." So they ran a fire hose down along his leg and turned it on. The water shot in and popped him right out. All I had to do was break the suction around Rick.

I had no fire hose, but I did have the water of the stream, and I jumped into it and held on to a branch. My own head was almost underwater, and the current kept pulling me downstream, but I fought against it and kept digging into the bank. I kept pulling out roots and stuff and digging and digging, but I did not seem to be making any headway until I had my arm dug into the bank almost to the armpit.

I wiggled my fingers forward stretching for Rick, and he said finally that he thought I had touched his leg. I cupped my hand and pulled out the last handful of muck between the stream and Rick. As I pulled my hand out, the water rushed in along Rick's leg and he bubbled to the surface up a column of rising water. The suction was broken and getting him out was only a matter of giving him a hand to pull against.

When he was out, he jumped in the stream to wash off the mud, and we laid our pants out to dry and went to sleep, knowing what we would have to do in the morning. We woke bright and early for it. A problem

like that could take us the whole day. We had dealt in-
dividually with the problem of taking risks. I knew what
Rick was going to say before he said it. Stalking Wolf
had told us that nature would never hurt us as long as
we went with it and did not panic. As long as we were in
tune with nature, we were invulnerable. The whole of
our belief system depended on the truth of that
statement. It was time to test the faith, and we both
knew it.

We walked out to the observation deck and leaped
into the mud. With a half an hour of wallowing and
wiggling, we both had ourselves as thoroughly stuck as
Rick had been the day before. It took us three hours to
figure it out, but once we did, it seemed too simple to
tell anybody about. Getting out was accomplished by
working one leg back and forth in short stiff-legged
motions until a working space had been created in the
mud. Each time we wiggled our knee around, we pushed
our rumps back further and further, creating a space
behind us as well. Eventually, we each got one knee
raised under muck. The rest was easy. We ran a hand
down to the knee, putting it palm down, and wiggled it
back and forth. The hand let in air as it went down, and
when it was moved, more air came in and broke the suction. Minutes later we were free.

We jumped in and did it again to check and make im-
provements in our technique but it seemed to be one of
those tricks that is so basic that it cannot be much improved in any important way. I must have used that
maneuver a dozen times since to get out of mud or
quicksand.

We got out of the mud caked with black ooze. Even
our faces were full of it. So we patted on more mud and
stuck leaves in it and walked up to the highway. We
stood at the side of the road, seeing how many people
would notice us. Not many did, and those that did
seemed to remember how lonely a road it was they were
on and sped away. Of all the ones who saw us and sped
away, not one had the curiosity to look back.

Compared to the morass those people were mired in,

afraid to look at what was around them, not the least curious about what there was that hadn't been seen yet or couldn't be explained, we had never been stuck. Whizzing along the highway with invisible blinders on, keeping their minds on the clock and their eyes on the road, they roared past us, late for supper or some appointment, tangled in obligations and duties, wrapped up in other people's schedules. They were more stuck than we had ever been, and if we had sunk in that mud until its thick viscosity had clogged our throats, we would still have been better off than the slowly smothering people who went by us.

There was clearly no quicksand as deep or hungry as a life among people, and what went by those who had sunk into the mud of their lives so long ago that they had become fossils. Rick and I turned away from the road and trudged back to camp. We dove into the stream again to wash off the taint of the highway more than the mud. The stream was colder than it had been before sunset, and it chilled us slightly. But while I lay shivering on the platform waiting to dry by the wind, I decided that, unlike the people we had seen go by in the cars, we could get free of our swamp, we could wriggle out and keep going. I was glad of that, and I would not have traded my goosebumps for some long-smothered driver's hot tub for anything in the world.

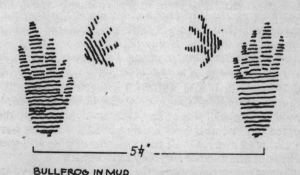

BULLFROG IN MUD

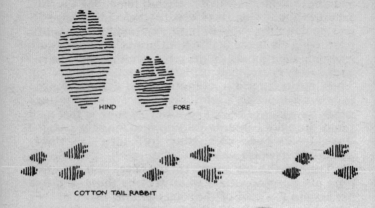

HIND   FORE

COTTON TAIL RABBIT

5/Cold Training

*I believe that Rick and I were out so often in the cold
that we became acclimated to it. Even now, I am comfortable outdoors in just a flannel shirt at ten above. It
may be an hereditary thing, some survival trait my line
of ancestors carried for the species and passed on to me.
Or it may be that fanatical curiosity just blots out
everything except whatever natural secret I'm trying to
unravel at the time. But whatever it is, Rick and I would
go into the winter woods wearing just our jeans, a flannel shirt, a sweater, and a jacket. Sometimes we wore as
many as four pairs of socks under our sneakers to keep
our feet warm, but at our most bundled up, we were
hardly dressed for the survival camping we often did in
the Pines.*

It wasn't that we didn't get cold, we just didn't *mind* it, and after a while, our bodies stopped reminding us that we were cold. I don't see how anybody could have a passion for nature without having an equally developed tolerance for the cold. Rick and I became immune to the cold because the things we wanted to know could only be known in the cold.

You cannot sit watching the Pines thicken with snow, or stand in the middle of a frozen lake at ten below watching the stars like kernels of frost forming in the frigid depths of the sky, if you care about being cold. You cannot see the sun burning gloves of frost off the pine needles as it rises in a January sky or understand the slow perpetual motion of the deer when even the soft brown pine needles are slivers of ice unless you have developed an indifference to cold.

We wanted to see those things. We wanted to *know*. So we learned an indifference to the cold so strong that we eventually came to prefer it. Being cold was always worth the price, whether it was to see minute catacombs of ice crystals on the banks of a frozen lake or to watch the rainbow-colored sheets of cloud that go up a January sky, pulling the best snowstorm of the winter up after them.

Because we sat and walked and slept in chronic cold, our bodies toughened our minds to it. Curiosity warmed us. Most of the time, we were too busy to be cold, too mystified and enraptured to feel the chill. We knelt in the snow for hours waiting for a muskrat to emerge from his hole. We lay on the ice looking down into it for some sign of fish. We stood in the swamp on brittle tufts of sphagnum watching the deer pick their way down the morning toward us. And every time, we were so surprised, or so awed, or so intrigued, that we felt nothing except the joy of the moment.

Stalking Wolf made the cold a rite of passage. He, Rick, and I were camped at the Good Medicine Cabin. Christmas had come and gone, and we had watched him deliver his New Year's prayer to the woods and to the spirit-that-moves-in-all-things. The weather was cold, but we had felt the warm, circling air go by us earlier and we knew that a snowstorm was coming. We did not know it was going to be a blizzard. I believe Stalking Wolf did.

We waited for the stories, nudging him with questions but he was silent, as if listening to counsel we could not hear. His father had been a medicine man, and he himself was a tracker. They listened to the same rhythms. Unwordable things seemed to be going on inside him. When he spoke, only his hand tried to articulate them. "This is a new year," he said, and the hand leveled the days the old year had knocked down. "You have done many things well." The hand danced our triumphs. "But there are things still to be done." The hand took up our destinies and held them waiting for time to strike a balance between them. "Give me your clothes."

I stood as quickly as Rick and began to take off my jacket. The hand went to sit ceremoniously in Stalking Wolf's lap. I pulled off the jacket and lay it at his feet. He did not smile. I took off the sweater as well. He did not move, and the hand did not rise to stop us. I took off my flannel shirt. The wind drew up close and ran its hands over my back. I shivered involuntarily. Stalking Wolf waited. My sneakers pulled one another from my feet, and I slid my pants down and stood before him in my underwear. My legs were speckled with cold, but my mind was free of it. The wind stuck fingers in through the walls, but I was too engrossed to notice. The question of what he would have us do was enormous; my mind could not leave it. The cold meant nothing next to the unanswered.

The ritual motion of Stalking Wolf's hands as he folded our clothes neatly and stood with them made me feel suddenly very solemn as if something important was about to happen, one of those things that so changes your life that the rest of it is forever different in some important way from what went before. Stalking Wolf reached into his bag and handed us each a pair of cutoffs. He allowed us to keep our sneakers. When we had put them on, he nodded and we sat down where we had been.

"The cold wind is your brother," he said. "You have treated him as your enemy." The hand rose in our defense. "If you go home in this fashion, you will never feel his bite again." Stalking Wolf's voice sounded as if going home was a journey we would make forever. The hand gave us its protection against our own weaknesses. The cold wind waited outside to meet us.

Stalking Wolf opened the door and Cold Wind poked his head in. The snow curled and settled to the floor like leaves. I watched it shave its gentle curves out of the air, touch the floor, and disappear. The flakes were large and falling thickly. I could see them coming down incessantly against the night. Stalking Wolf sealed the door and was gone.

Rick and I waited until he would have been well on his way and then stepped outside into the snow. The sheer beauty of it made us warm, and we set off along the trail as if it was spring and walking home was as easy as staying where we were. Cold Wind met us on the trail where we least expected him. He came with a thickening of the snow, and we felt him kicking up the branches before he began to whirl the snow around us.

There was more to his touch than we imagined, and we began to shiver long before I would have expected us to. There was still a long walk home ahead of us, and the snow was painting the deer trails and the dog runs white, like highways between the darker masses of the trees. But from the ground, everything had begun to look the same, and only the fact that we had come that way so often kept us moving as we should. The further we went, the tighter the wind held the swirls of snow to us until we could hardly see where we were going.

Before half way I had begun to feel truly cold. My body shivered freely and without restraint. My capacity for cold seemed to lessen with each step. I felt as if water were running down inside my skin, wetting it and leaving me vulnerable to the cold. Moving tried to warm me, but I had been too cold too long. My teeth began to chatter. We were still three miles from the house. The cold wind kept telling me to lie down and rest. I wanted to speak to Rick, but my voice would not work. My mouth could not form the words. My voice was a shiver.

I felt our brother, the icy wind, lay his heaviest hand against us. The wind wrapped us in a cocoon of flakes. There seemed no way I could go on. I was so cold that all the times I had been cold before seemed to have accumulated and been given to me to endure at once. A mile further on, Cold Wind touched us for the last time. The chill that surrounded me wrapped tighter.

The snow was up over the top of our sneakers. My feet burned when I walked. Every step seemed to form me in ice and break me loose to take the next step. If we had come that far lost and afraid, we would have died. But we were on an adventure Stalking Wolf had planned for us. I thought about what he had always told us, that nature could not hurt us if we were at one with it, and I stopped resisting the cold. The result was instantaneous. Cold Wind seemed to laugh through the pines, shaking down snow in its passage. My coldness was gone.

I took another few steps without feeling it. Only when I looked at Rick did I realize that I was warm again, that the cold had left me never to return. We quickened our pace, anxious to get home and tell Stalking Wolf what had happened. We were running by the time we reached Stalking Wolf's house, and laughing, and scooping up huge handfuls of snow and throwing them on each other. The wind died for a while, and we ran through the break in the storm toward Stalking Wolf's house. When we stepped inside, the house seemed uncomfortably hot. Stalking Wolf met us smiling and gave us back our clothes. I have not been truly cold since.

MINK

6/Night Crawl

Summer woods were always more than magical. The swamp near the cabin was busy as a shopping center. Things came and went, ate and were eaten. And we watched it all, sitting motionless on the observation deck while a Great Blue Heron came in over the last few trees before the swamp, out of a sunset that was all oranges and golds with a low roll of clouds at the horizon to catch the color and show it off. He was like a great galley ship, his wings rowing him through the air in long powerful beats; his long neck curved back proudly toward his body as if he knew that nothing in the swamp looked half as majestic.

His legs stretched back behind him like streamers blown almost horizontal by the power of his flight. When he landed, his huge wings seemed to fan slowly forward until they almost touched. He stood in the shallows on thin, frail legs that looked like accessories stuck onto a creature that was never really meant to touch the ground. He uncoiled his neck and cocked his head as if trying to decide which delicacy to choose and, like a snake, the neck coiled again and struck.

His bill went into the water and back out in a flash, spearing a frog and squeezing it between its narrow points. Then he tossed the frog into his mouth, gave a hoarse croak and looked again. He fished another half hour before he moved so far out in the swamp that we couldn't see him any more. Rick and I had not moved since we saw him coming in over the trees—gliding, stroking, gliding. There was something in the grace of his motion that would not let us sit still, and we moved through the twilight woods away from the cabin. We had no goal and no direction. There was a long, high cloud to the south-east just catching the last of the sun on its underside. It looked like a rock placed too close to the fire. We moved in the direction of the cloud.

A mile or two south, at the edge of an open meadow, we found wild irises, and by the time we had stopped examining them, it was full dark. We sat at the edge of the field looking up at the stars as they came out, clear and bright, the way they look reflected in an unfrozen lake during a winter lull. There had been tracks at the edge of the iris bed, the two dots and two exclamation marks of a huge rabbit we had come to think of as the Rabbit King because he was so big.

But if was too dark to follow the trail into the grass, so we sat where we were twirling shafts of grass between our fingers and wishing we could track the Rabbit King. We had seen his tracks before. We found them there every day we came by, but we could never see the rabbit that made them.

The movement of animals is as full of personal quirks as the movement of people. The question of where he came from and how, could have no answer until we tracked him. But the Rabbit King only came out at night and when I said we should track him, Rick wanted to know how we could track him if we couldn't see his tracks. Stalking Wolf had given me the answer to that weeks before. He had mentioned night tracking, and I asked him how he could track in the dark. He told me to close my eyes and walk to the door without breaking anything. "We'll feel track!" I told Rick.

We spent the next few hours crawling around in the grass looking for a rabbit run. Mammals are habitual animals; they set up their routines and they don't vary them very much; the Rabbit King was the same. He had come through the field for months, down the same paths over and over again, until he had worn himself a runway down near the bottom of the grass that the tops of the grass closed over and hid. Even in the daylight we would have had to follow his tracks into one of his runs to find it. With feel tracking, it was only a matter of time before we found it, and eventually we did.

What was invisible to our eyes was plain as it could be to our hands. Alongside the run, there was a double wall of grass that had come back up after being trampled. But the grass in the run itself was permanently pushed down or worn away entirely. We traced the run to others, and within a couple hours, we had his main routes established and we had found his favorite feeding grounds. All we had to do was wait.

We lay at the side of the run leading to his favorite eating place and put our faces right next to the path. Then we wove grass up along our faces and tied it over our heads so that we looked through a parted curtain of grass onto the run. We had to wait another two hours, but eventually, the Rabbit King came down the trail that almost touched our noses.

I had seen bigger rabbits, but not wild, and if I had been a dog, I would have thought twice about attacking him if he was cornered. He seemed to sense something and he stopped a couple feet from us. He looked around, seemed to shrug it off, and hopped forward. He stopped again right in front of us. I don't know whether he didn't see us or if he saw us and didn't believe what he saw, but he sat there between our faces and wrinkled his nose. He looked like somebody just beginning to figure out that they're on "Candid Camera."

Rick started to giggle, and the rabbit thumped and took off. I jumped up with a howl. In taking off, the Rabbit King had brought that big rear foot down across my nose, leaving a long red scratch. We congratulated ourselves on having tracked the Rabbit King and marveled at having been so close to him. Rick made faces like the rabbit when he first seemed to realize that there were human heads not six inches away from him. For a moment it had seemed as if he was ignoring us, hoping we'd go away.

I rolled over laughing at Rick's rabbit imitations and when we had tired of laughing, Rick suggested we feel track the rest of the field and see what we could find. I agreed and we began crawling again.

We were out in the middle of the field when I hit an alleyway in the grass that was far too wide to be a rabbit run. The excitement galloped through me. It was a highway made by the passing bodies of deer and it was recently worn.

I started to follow it, and I had gone no more than a couple feet when I felt a track being pressed out of shape by the heel of my hand. Even though it was dark, I closed my eyes and concentrated on what my fingers were feeling. Everywhere I put my hand I could feel deer tracks! It was all that I could do not to jump up and start shouting for Rick.

Instead, I gave the muffled croak of a tree frog and kept it up until Rick came crawling in from behind me. I took his wrist and put his hand down on the tracks, and I could feel the elation when his fingers touched it and he realized what it was. We crawled down the run single file until it widened out and we lost it. We crawled in a circle looking for it but all we found was a clearing within the field.

It dawned on me finally that we were in the middle of the area where the deer were currently coming to graze. The grass was almost lawn short in a lot of places compared with the knee high grass everywhere else in the field. Rick crawled up beside me and asked if I had had any luck. I whispered that I thought we were in the middle of a feeding area. There was no need to say that they would be back before the night was over. We crawled into the half grazed grass and lay on our backs, looking up at the sky.

We kept motionless, and only the feet of the Jersey Devil coming down on both sides of our head would have caused either of us to make a sound. We lay for an hour looking up into the black, star-filled sky until at some point, although I never closed my eyes, I was no longer lying in a field. I had become part of a pattern that the stars and the breeze and the grass and the insects were all part of. There was no awareness of this until I heard the first deer coming through the grass. Then I was suddenly aware that I had been lying there without thoughts or sensations other than just *being*.

I had felt like that before, but I had always reasoned that I had just dozed off, but it had been hours since I had been aware of myself, and yet I knew everything that had gone on around me. I had heard the rushes and lulls of the crickets and had seen a bat and a nighthawk go across the stars. But I had not made the distinction between what was happening and myself. It was the second wonder of the night, and I felt my body tense with the anticipation of the third.

There wasn't much of a breeze and our scent was all over the field if it was anywhere at all, but the deer came cautiously when they came. The buck had apparently discounted what he could catch of our scent as a residual from the day. He must have told himself that we couldn't possibly be there and just kept on coming down his habitual road in the grass to his favorite dinner.

I held my breath and the stars disappeared inside an enormous silhouette. The buck stood between Rick and me and bent its head down to graze. When I have seen something in nature that I know almost no one else has seen or experienced, it gives me an elation that I can hardly contain. I wanted to jump up and shout I was so happy.

The most difficult animal in the woods to hunt was so close that we could have rolled our heads over and leaned them against his cheek. Above me the stars seemed to be singing, weaving spells of invisibility. I believe now that while we were lying there in that field, we had so immersed ourselves in that moving pattern of nature Stalking Wolf always seemed to be watching that we were truly invisible to the deer and could have lain in the same position at high noon without being seen. The buck chewed with deafening regularity next to my ear, and I could see the stars again as he swung away and stepped across Rick.

About halfway across him, the deer caught his scent and froze. Then it jumped back away from Rick and I almost gasped waiting for one of those sharp hooves to come poking down through my chest with the weight of a prancing 150 pound deer behind it. One of the back legs went over me, and then the other, as if he were backing slowly away from Rick. But he caught my scent halfway across me as well and started forward between Rick and me again. Then he seemed to go crazy. He would step across Rick and pull back, and then back almost into me and jerk forward. The logs his mind had been jumping back and forth over had ceased to be logs but had not yet coalesced into boys.

In his growing panic, he began jumping back and forth over us, not knowing what to do when he landed but to jump away from the new threat. The stars flared and flashed with every step the deer took over me. He went back and forth over us perhaps three times, but it seemed like he was dancing those sharp hooves across us for days. Once, a foot went down right beside my head. I lay as if dead.

Getting up would only have started him kicking, and rolling away was as likely to put me under his hooves as lying steady where I was. At least there, he knew where I was and wanted to avoid stepping on me.

I think Rick started to laugh out of nervousness or

sheer outrageousness, and the deer flexed between us and shot off up into the darkness so powerfully that I almost thought he was going to disappear into the stars.

The first time he had stepped back, the stars had disappeared completely and for an instant, I thought that perhaps he had stepped on me, killing me instantly, and I was lying there dead watching the rest of it. But he moved off, and the stars had come shining back, and the whole thing was so incredibly beautiful that I did not care if I was alive or dead as long as it didn't stop.

We heard the deer thrash away through the higher grass, startling other deer a little further away with incredible news. If we had jumped up, we might have seen a dozen dark shapes bounding away through the grass toward the tree line. But neither of us could move, and it was a long long time before either of us spoke. When we did, there did not seem to be anything that could be said.

We became fanatical feel trackers for a while. Every time we found a trail, we would close our eyes and see if we could follow it just by feeling the tracks and judging where the next one should be. Sometimes Rick would blindfold me and lead me to the beginning of a trail and let me go. I would crawl along it like a blind man letting my fingers see what was there. Eventually, we could follow a trail that way if we had to and after years and years, I could tell a great deal just from the feeling of a track.

The problem was that unless it was done very delicately, feeling destroyed the track, and whenever we found a really interesting trail at night, we tried to let it go until daylight. At one time we tried to go through our entire day blindfolded, but we were not very good at it. Toward afternoon, I began to get the hang of it by doing everything very meticulously and reducing everything I could to a routine. But, by and large, we couldn't even break up the sticks for the fire without more difficulty than it was worth, and we took off the blindfolds, deciding that while it could be done if necessary, it was not something that was worth spending

time on. The winter after that, however, I wished we
had persevered.

Rick was away, as he often was, and I was camping
alone in a section of the Pine Barrens we called the
"desert," a four or five square mile area without trees
and basically without water. I camped about two hundred yards out toward the center of a bubble off the
main body of the desert, and I spent a long day out there
watching the flight of winter birds. I had made a lean-to
out of branches dragged out there from the tree line,
and I wakened briefly in the night to the fact that it was
snowing.

The next morning there were about four inches on the
ground. It was light and wet and made for tracking. It
was the kind of thing I would fantasize about, a snowy
day where the tracks of everything would be clearer than
they would be again until the next snowfall. The temperature had gone up and the storm was gone. The
animals were beginning to come down and get the
necessities the snowstorm had kept them from earlier in
the day. In an hour, they would be like people out shopping the day after the snow, when the roads are finally
clear enough to take a chance. There were tracks
everywhere. It was a feast.

I bounded up out of my sleeping bag and started
tracking almost before the sun was up, going over the
ground and running down each trail into the woods.
The best resolution to a trail is the animal that made it,
and Rick and I always hoped when we started down one
that we would find at the end of it the actual physical
mystery of the animal itself.

It was a coup and a triumph to find one, but it was
not the usual occurrence. Usually, the trail would wind
around in circles and meander back and forth, and by
the time we had traced all its convolutions, the animal
was long gone. Still, we knew that if we pursued it,
eventually, even if it took years, we would come to the
animal that had made the tracks. We would find tracks
with feet still in them.

When we found the animal and were discovered, the

animal always seemed to give us a look of incredulity just before it bolted. I found half a dozen surprised squirrels that day, and a rabbit that had ducked under a drift of snow piled up against a log until the storm had stopped. But the most fantastic track of all came around noon. I found at the edge of the tree line, running out from it into the desert, the single line of tracks that meant a fox had been there.

In my mind, I watched him go, one foot in front of the other, like a dotted line out into the treeless plain. I followed that trail almost laughing with joy at my good fortune. The fox is the hardest animal there is to track, and the chance of following one right up to its feet was slim. But there were the tracks, clear as they could be, and I knew that if I followed them I would eventually come to the fox.

I read the tracks near the wood line, and I could see the fox as a red streak leaping to a skidding stop as a rabbit made a sharp right turn on him and dove into the briars. His tracks went around the tangle of briars for a while and then went jogging off in the snow across the desert.

I backtracked him a bit and found that the rabbit had been a lucky accident, and the fox had really been on his way somewhere else. In fact, he seemed to be in a hurry or else he was well fed, because he did not seem to have spent nearly long enough investigating the hiding place of the rabbit. I wondered what it could be that would make a fox give up the chase so easily and start across the desert in such a straight and certain line.

I went after it squinting into the white light of the snow to pick up the tracks that went straight only a few hundred feet before they started taking the secret evasive action of a fox in a vulnerable place. The trail was full of turns and counterturns and oddities of behavior that I couldn't decipher without watching the fox actually making the tracks. I wished I had been there when he had come by to see what it was that he did when the prints made indicipherable little stutters from place to place.

Everything of interest was circled and observed before he moved in close for a more thorough investigation, and I spent hours trying to figure out what he had done. I was about halfway along his trail and a good way into the afternoon when a sudden wind blew snow in my eyes and they began to water so much that I couldn't see the track. But I didn't want to give it up, so I followed it on my hands and knees, wiping the water out of my eyes until my cheeks got chapped from the cold, and I had to sit down and rest my eyes. I wanted to find that fox so badly that I couldn't think of anything else. But secretly I knew what was happening to me, and I lied to myself that I could go back to my camp and warm up and eat something and come back to the track fresh.

I knew that if I went back, any hope of coming upon the fox himself would be gone. So I went back to the trail, blinking and squinting and getting down so close to it that I was almost feeling my way along. Finally, when I couldn't see the tracks because my eyes were tearing so much, I sat back and tried to orient myself again.

I had been down with the track so long and I was having such a hard time seeing it, that I had not checked where the trail was going. When I finally did, I found that he had led me in a big circle back past my camp. Undoubtedly, the rest of the trail went back into the woods to where he lived. I was about fifty yards from my camp but I could only vaguely see it, and I was surprised when I walked toward it, that it was not a mile or so away but only a few hundred feet.

My eyes were still watering as I made my fire, and they stung so much that there was nothing to do but crawl into my sleeping bag and abandon the fox until the next day. I told myself I could still follow him then, but I knew that it was unlikely. Still, there was nothing to do about it, and my eyes hurt; so I curled up in my sleeping bag in the lean-to and kept the fire going until I fell asleep. When I woke up the next morning I was blind.

I had heard vaguely of snowblindness. It was not common in New Jersey and I did not think to identify it as that. Instead, I assumed that I had permanently burned out some part of my eyes as surely as if I had been staring into the sun. Still, I was not in total darkness; I could see vague shapes, a shifting blurriness, and dark patches I assumed must be the tree line. I shouted at it to see how far away it was, the echo came back quick. Still it looked like miles. It was impossible to go home that way. I might, in absolute desperation, have tried to feel track my way backwards to a highway, but the snow had covered my earlier tracks and I would have no sure way.

I could no more see the firewood than an out-of-focus camera, and I would have been unable to see any low hanging branches if I had tried to walk out. There was a half mile of Pine Barrens wilderness once I got out of the desert, before I could come to a major trail, and any misstep along the way would send me wandering as helplessly as any lost hunter.

I decided to wait for Rick. If I was not back by Monday, he would come looking for me, and he would know where to look even if I had not told him where I would be. And if Rick could not find me, Stalking Wolf, reading the secret pattern of the woods, would find me easily. I sat where I was and closed my eyes, hoping they would heal themselves in the darkness but doubting that they would ever focus again.

If no one showed up by Wednesday and my eyes had not gotten better, I would have to think of getting myself out. I tried to remember when I had been able to see clearly last to see if I could establish some time frame for how long my blindness would last, if it was not already irreversible. I remembered looking at a snowdrift. The wind was blowing crystals of ice off it, and the waviness of the top of it gave it an up-and-down motion that made it look like ghosts riding by as the wind blew across it. I could almost see the shapes of an Indian war party in the swirl of snow as they galloped along the top of the snowbank and then veered into a column left where the bank dropped off at the down-wind end and set the snow spiraling to the left. The stronger the wind blew, the faster they rode, and when they jerked their ponies to the left, the heels of the ponies seemed to kick up the ice that blew back into my eyes.

At first, I thought that the ice had gotten into my eye and had frozen some trivial part of the lens and I persisted in wiping my eyes, waiting for what I thought was the numbness to go away and continue to track against the brilliantly white snow.

The snowbank warriors were a warning I should have heeded. When I had first lifted my head toward the snowbank, the sun was hitting the blowing snow in a way that made it shine with a painful dazzling brilliance. I should have known then that the snow was blinding me, and I cursed my stupidity for getting so caught up in watching those wind ghosts that I did not think to look beyond them. Still, I thought, if that had been my last sight, it was certainly a powerful one to take with me into the darkness.

There were ghost Indians in the snowfield of my vision as I sat in front of my fire without opening my eyes. But even keeping the flame small, I used up all the fuel I had before noon. The air would be warming for another two or three hours, and then it would begin to cool rapidly into the night. I had no idea how long it would take to crawl to the tree line and back, so I began when the fire died.

The tree line ran two thirds of a lopsided circle around the camp, and I wanted to pick the shortest route; so, I moved around the tent shouting and listening for the resound from the woods. When I believed I had found the shortest route, I began to crawl across the snow. It was shading past the brightest part of the day, and even opening my eyes made them sting. I tried to go along closing my eyes and crawling straight ahead for a few feet before I opened them for another peek in the direction of the tree line.

I looked through squinted eyes, but the glare made my eyes hurt too much even in short bursts for me to look very often. I kept my eyes closed and crawled longer each time before I opened them again. I went further than I should have a couple times and had to make sharp turns in the furrow I was crushing in the snow. I consoled myself each time with the thought that they would be useful landmarks when I crawled back.

Going out was difficult, but gathering the twigs was even harder. Trees blurred into themselves as I got close and twigs were never really visible. I had to feel for small bushes and break off the dry branches or feel around for sticks still above the snow line. I did not end up with a huge armload to crawl back with, and I had to make two more trips. But with the crawl trail broken in the snow, it was a lot easier and I could keep my eyes closed most of the time.

Finally, I had enough wood to last the coldest part of the day and night. I tried and tried to focus on close objects but the act of doing it felt intolerably grotesque, as if I was twisting my face out of shape every time I opened my eyes. Trying to focus made my eyes ache, and I gave up on it after a while and went entirely by feel. It was easier than it might have been if we had never tracked that way, but it was still difficult most of the time.

The fire should have been hard to start, but I was lucky and the tinder caught just as quickly as it would have if I had been able to see it. I turned my gloves inside out and put them on my eyes to keep them warm. I sat or lay and listened to the sounds of the day that I had not been able to listen to before. There was an erratic wind blowing that hissed and slashed across the surface of the snow. I could hear long snakes of loose snow slither before it into the wood line.

In the woods, it rattled the tufts of pine and shook down long whispers of snow. It passed a vague finger sputtering into my fire and tufted the pine needles of the lean-to with a whirling sound I had never noticed before. I believe the fox came back late in the day to take a look. I think I heard him, but the snow was gone before I got back there to see.

By night, I could hear the changes in the way the cold cracked the crust of the snow, and I believe that if I had stayed until morning, I could have heard the movements of the clouds and the spinning of the stars. But somewhere in the early evening my sight started to come back, and by midnight I could see well enough to make it a good bet I could find my way out. The snow gave just enough outline to see by and I packed my stuff and began to walk.

I was afraid at first that I might strain my eyes and have them give out on me part of the way to the road, but my eyes got better in the dim light and by the time I got home I could see almost normally. As I left the desert, the wind galloped the ghost Indians up over the crest of a trailside snowbank. I could see them for a second, galloping toward me full of menace, but they reined in as the wave of snow died down at mid-bank. They swirled in the snow for a second and then went galloping back off down the snowbank to invisibility. I had no doubt after that that I would make it home.

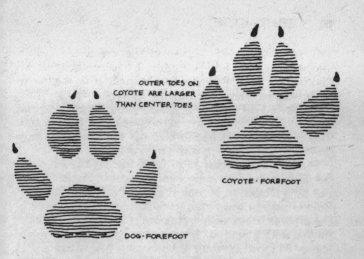

OUTER TOES ON
COYOTE ARE LARGER
THAN CENTER TOES

COYOTE · FOREFOOT

DOG · FOREFOOT

7/The Dog Tree

I came to the Dog Tree after noon. It was not called that then, but it was a landmark to us nevertheless. Rick had gone away for a week, and I was alone in the woods, freed for three days or more by an Easter-week vacation. I had come out early, watching the sun come up red and misty out of the trees across the river. The birds were everywhere, grackles, swifts, robins. Near the far bank of the lake on the way into the woods, I saw two pairs of Canadian geese on their way back from an extended southern vacation. Flowers were coming out everywhere, and the trees seemed to have put out extra buds during the night. At almost every step, there was something that could not be passed up.

Cottontails sprang like lunatics from the path, tumbling over themselves in impossible escapes, making fantastic twisting leaps as if the jaws of death closed just behind

their tails. I should have seen the omen in it, but
everything was so full of life that I had no thoughts of
the intricate web of hunter and hunted. If dogs moved
in the woods, they were moving quietly, and the birds
sang instead of scolding. Everything seemed newly
created. Greenery thickened between the Pines, and
open places where I had looked off the trail deep into
the woods were filled in with growing things.

The trail was a highway of fresh tracks, and I moved
forward following one after another, or backtracking to
pick up a fresh one. It took the whole morning to reach
the camp, and I was buzzing with things seen and heard.
The air was heavy with spring and the scent of animals
moving with abandon. Everywhere I looked, a branch
bent or whipped skyward as birds came and went.

I did not see the Red Tailed Hawk until I was almost
to the camp. Perhaps I should have known then that it
was a time of adventure. I watched the hawk move
down the sky until I lost him in the tops of the trees. He
seemed exhilarated, as if he had just done something of
great magnitude, and he cut the air with a folded wing
and dove at nothing for the sheer joy of diving. I stood a
long time watching the empty sky where the mark of his
flight seemed to linger almost visibly. It was a good day,
a prize day.

The river branch dove left and then right, cutting an
arrowhead of land at its bend. The tree stood a little
inland, pushing out buds as if some force inside it
demanded release. A log bridge straddled the river
where it narrowed to a stream along the north side of
the arrowhead. Up the path beyond it was Stoney Hill
with its Indian relics. Later, I expected to go up that
way, but there was a camp to make first and fish to
catch and eat.

I lay my pack and my burlap bag of food in the
clearing and looked for forked branches to make a spit.
A bass broke above the fast running water beneath the
log. I thought I would go and sit on the log later and
watch him for a while so that I could know him before I

put my hook in. I wanted to let him know that what I did, I did not out of malice but to live.

But I wanted to prepare the fire first and the spit. The morning excitement had sharpened my appetite, and I scouted the underbrush near the base of the tree for the right sticks. I wanted them identical with a little fork on one side to lay the cross piece in. I wanted to see the fish spitted, his head still intact and take in the last of his beauty before I ate.

I knew his color and his size already. I knew his taste. He was my fish, my food from the moment I saw him, just as the fly had been his food while he was still circling under the rushing water. Somewhere he was making a tight turn into the short, powerful run before his leap. Later, that leap for lunch would make him my lunch as well. Things were as they should be. The woods moved in its complex rhythm, things mated and bred, ate and were eaten. The whole was sustained by the interlocking network of its parts.

I liked where the camp was. I could look across the log bridge and up a wide trail to where the ground rose with trees on both sides and the path disappeared down the other side of the rise. When I looked up it, a chickadee whistled across the path from tree to tree. I looked back at the tendrils of branch I was stripping from the uprights of my spit, saving them for the second layer of the fire. I piled them to one side and held the twigs up against one another. They were fine.

I thought maybe I would go up the path later and find some berries for dessert. Cold Pine Barrens water was hardly ten feet away filled with life, running swift and clear as if fifty miles to the north other rivers were not caked with chemicals and sewage. I stuck the uprights in the ground and began to build the fire, weaving the tiniest twigs with a hierarchy of larger branches that would guide the fire up and along the fish.

It was a ritual meant to make anyone, who carried it out meticulously, cherish what he was about to eat. It made the bass the center of my day. My world turned around him, and the Pine Barrens turned around me, spinning the continent outward around the curve of the globe. I could almost feel the stars turning in a great invisible wheel above the high blueness of the sky, and for an instant, we spun together, the stars, the river, the fish, and me.

When I looked up the trail, the dogs were already scrambling down the near side of the rise. I felt the scar on my lip tingle.

It was only a short run to the log and across it, and if the first dog across had not bumped the second and gone splashing into the water, they would have torn me down before I reached the lowest branch of the tree. I looked around before I stood, searching for the best tree within reach, but the big tree near the water was the only one I could be sure of making, and I sprang toward it.

The lead dog swept around the point of the land yelping and struggling against the current. It occurred to me that he might not make it out, and I wished him into the fastest part of the current where his legs would tire and let him drown. The other five hesitated on the far side of the log for a second, watching their leader shrieking downstream. His terror seemed to disarm them for a moment, and it gave me the time I needed.

The lowest branch was a good twelve feet off the ground, and I cupped my arms around the trunk like a logger's safety belt and ran up whipping my locked hands up before me on the far side of the tree. I had a hand on the lowest branch and then another before the first dog leaped. He had left the ground too soon, and he dropped short as I swung up onto the branch. The other four dogs tumbled in behind him, leaping and snarling. But I was well beyond their reach and they knew it.

My heart was pounding, but it was more from the thrill of the adventure than from fear. I looked down and a shiver ran through me as first one dog, then another threw themselves upward, their lips curled back along their teeth. I thought of what wonderful skulls they would leave as their final track.

No doubt, they thought of *my* skull, cracking like a

nut in the narrowing angle of their jaws, opening the sweet delicacy of my brain to them like the meat of a walnut. I could see their hunger in the joyous frenzy of their leaps. They wanted me with a sadistic exuberance that made them keep leaping long after they had any chance of reaching me. I looked away from them up the tree for a comfortable place to sit.

As I climbed, they knocked each other out of the way with the jumping as if they thought they might scare me into a misstep that would drop me among them like tossed meat. Even when I got to the comfortable fork of a higher branch, far up near the top of the tree, they continued barking and howling. For the moment, I was the spinning center of their world.

I adjusted my back against the trunk and dangled my legs. To my left, I could see the first dog dragging himself out of the water a hundred yards downstream. His yelping had become a sullen silence. He shook himself and looked back at the water with a useless snarl. The river rushed on oblivious. I smiled. There was so much to see from where I sat; the river wound like a canyon down between the trees. Birds moved over the tops of other trees so close they seemed to tip the topmost leaves. A squirrel went from the tip on one branch to another across the rolling tops of the trees whose tiniest branches seemed to interlock in a vast highway whose existence I had not even guessed at. The view alone was worth the climb.

I put the view aside for a while and looked down at the dogs. Some of them ran back and forth along my scent from the unlit campfire to the tree, back and forth as if they expected me to suddenly appear in the middle of my spoor and give myself over to them. Others barked but had stopped leaping at the trunk of the tree. One leaned cautiously out over the water as if there had been some mistake, and I had disappeared under the water instead of up the tree. The Alpha dog sent them howling and leaping at the bottom of the tree again. I sat back and watched, thanking the spirit of the woods for my ringside seat to the dog show.

After a longer while than I expected, they turned to collect my admission. The lead dog tore open the burlap bag, ignoring the pack, and scattered the cans as he shook the bag in his teeth. The others dove for the cans and bit into them. I had seen cans at the dump shredded and scraped for the last morsels of food, but I had never seen it done firsthand before. I sat delighted with the show. They bit through the cans, the big dogs biting and sliding the can back further in their mouths. I couldn't see how they kept the metal from slicing up between their teeth, but they did.

I waited patiently for a couple of them to chew themselves into casualties, but they didn't. In a way I was glad, although I hated them for their viciousness and would have killed them gladly if I could, if only in return for the shambles they had made of my dreams from time to time. If the three biggest had ruined themselves on the cans, I might have been able to come down and drive the other three away. But as I watched them work the tattered cans in their jaws, I knew there was no hope of that. I was stuck in the tree until they got bored and went away. I reconciled myself to that and looked around.

The fish moved as dark shapes under the water. Ants made a highway along the trunk and I put my face up against the tree to see them walking the tiny ravine in the bark, full of dedication and purpose. I wondered if there was one ant in the column going steadily by that let its curiosity distract it from its job and set it wandering down some curling side road in the formic acid, hot on the trail of some mystery.

But I never saw one that didn't stay within the lane of formic acid laid down by some functionary between the nest and food. One or two got lost and did a large erratic circle as big as my hand, like some hunter from the city trying to find the jeep trail he has wandered off. The rest never went far wrong before they stopped and circled, looking for the trail. They did not seem comfortable until they found it again.

The ones I took in my hand explored their new world

looking for their old; I doubt that they saw much. When I put them back down on the trunk of the tree, they blended right back into the flow of commuters if I put them down near the trail. If I put them down in a new part of the tree, they searched with ferocious diligence until they found the highway again, the road to home, job, and duty.

I decided that they were depressingly like people in the end, but I admired the way they tracked, even if I didn't like their purpose. Whenever they lost the trail, they stopped where they were and traced a rectangle right and left, front and back until they found their center point again. If they couldn't find the trail, they went back to their center point and circled around it in widening circles until they picked up the scent. The more familiar they were with the territory, the smaller the circles.

It was the way Stalking Wolf had taught me to look for a lost trail. I drew the same right/left baseline as the ant, took a stride right, and semicircled left around the point of the last track. When I hit the baseline, I took another stride, this time to the left, and semi-circled back to the right. Already at twelve, I had drawn that backward-folding semicircular maze more times than I could count, searching for vanished trails I knew must be there somewhere. Maybe in the long run, I thought, I was an ant myself and the Pine Barrens was my pine tree.

I fantasized that among the ants, there might be one who had trained himself so thoroughly that he could roam the entire tree and find his way back without any official road of formic acid to tell him the way to civilization. Specialized as a queen, he would perform his function, wandering the tree, putting lost ants back on the nearest trail. I wanted to be an ant like that.

I thought what a great thing it would be if there really was an ant like that. I could see him with an incredible joy in his work, wandering, wandering, wandering the infinitely variable bark of his tree, following every mystery to its hiding place, examining the skulls of everything that passed, noting everything, enlarging his own vision of the tree.

But the sun went down, and I lost the ants in the changing contour of the tree. The darkness came in like a tide, shade by shade, deepening the water into space and throwing the stars back with the roll of its seaward motion. I don't know how long I watched the canyon of the trees, where the branch followed its obsession to the river itself and to the Atlantic. The stream deepened and receded down the darkening tunnel of my vision.

I watched the river dim, darken, and then come slowly bright again as my eyes adjusted to the dark. The woods grew in my eyes. The river grew in the woods. The stars grew in the river. Everything was so different and so new from where I was sitting that I would not have gone down out of the tree even if the six shapes beneath it had vanished without saying goodbye.

I took off my extra long Boy Scout belt, understanding for the first time why they insisted on selling them so big, and fastened myself to the branch with my belly against the trunk. Down my left shoulder, the river got lighter and lighter as the moon rose, and the stars sent their messages between high misty clouds down through the branches to me.

In fits and starts, I fell sleep and woke to changes, cursing myself for missing them. Sometimes when I awoke, I got hungry, but that passed. Then I got thirsty, and that didn't. So I put it aside until I could do something about it and watched the sun come up and the dogs jerking and twitching in their dreams.

I wondered if they were dreaming about me; how my fine soft skin would tear, how much I would fight. I didn't think they thought they had anything more powerful than a house cat up the tree, and I got suddenly angry to be taken that much for granted. There were those stupid dogs lying down under the tree like I was some up-state hunter moaning over a little discomfort and crying to be let down.

By the time the anger got to be righteous indignation, I had untied myself and had quietly broken off a dozen wrist-thick branches, bending them back to their breaking point and working them loose. There were plenty of dead branches in the tree, and I had a stack of them in the neck of the branch when I sat back down and hooked my legs around the trunk.

The lead dog was stretched out at the base of the tree, down and to my right. The others were various distances away, like a platoon sleeping at ease but keeping up the social distances. The Alpha dog lay alone, nearest the tree, first to claim the juiciest portion. I could see him dreaming of my skull in his nutcracker mouth, and I threw the first log with the accuracy of blind fury.

I knew from the thump that I had hit him someplace good and hard, and the yelp that followed it sounded dazed. But the snarl and the attack that followed it told me he wasn't an animal to go down easy, and I respected him for that. I could see vague shapes at the bottom of the tree when they moved, and the sounds told me that the Alpha dog had jumped up and attacked the nearest dog, who then yelped and launched a counterattack.

The other dogs were up and barking. I leaned down to see better, and the dark shape at the base of the tree got suddenly larger as the lead dog came hurtling upward. I jerked back even though he was far below me and grabbed a stick to fight him off with. Lifted by his rage, he must have come uncomfortably close to that first branch, and I had a vision of him clamping onto it with his teeth and working his way up the tree bite by bite.

Gradually the bark and growl died to a mutter, and the dogs settled back down. I watched the darkness for a while until they got to sleep again and then fired down another log. There was a softer thump, a fractional pause, and a yipe that set the rest to snarling and growling. I knew that I had gotten one of them on the bounce. The third log hit nothing but ground, and I knew they had moved off out of sight. So I let them go until morning, proud of myself for my generosity.

I watched the sun come up through thickening clouds, red and purple. The dogs got up soon after. The Alpha dog came back to the bottom of the tree cautiously, almost formally. I threw a log down at him, but he jumped back as my arm went up. "The next time he comes," I thought, "I'll have it raised so he has less time to react." He backed off and barked. I shook the stick at him, but outside of a slight flinch the first time, he didn't budge.

I could tell by looking at him that he was one of those rare wild dogs that would attack alone if he had to. Three dogs or less will usually leave a single hiker alone; six or less will leave two people alone, unless they panic. He was not one to be scared off or bored off either, and the others would stay as long as he stayed, or until they got a riskless chance to run away.

I watched the way he moved, and the way his movements moved the other dogs. I knew a lot about him before the sun got all the way up, and by noon I believed I knew how to beat him in the end. I spent the rest of the day driving him crazy.

I crawled around in the tree until I found a place where I could stand and hang on and still have space to throw. Then I began to fire what sticks I had left at him. I broke off some smaller ones and threw all the badly shaped ones first so that they thought my range was a lot shorter than it was.

Eventually they moved in, cautiously, I threw another stick short, and they gave it a respectful distance but moved well within range. I went back to watching the commuters go up and down the tree, naming each species to myself, and then renaming them with my own name. There were nine species of Tom Brown's Beetle on that tree.

Every once in a while, I'd underchuck a stick until they had stopped raising their heads when they heard it whizz through the air. Then I stood up again and went back up further in the tree and threw my heaviest stick with everything I had at that second dog. It couldn't have been more than halfway there when I threw the next one. The first stick hit the Beta dog on the rump and woke him with a yelp that raised the head of the Alpha dog just enough for the second stick to hit him a glancing blow on the thick fur of his neck.

The rest of the dogs scrambled backwards, but the Alpha dog charged toward the tree, until I landed one close to him about halfway in. He veered off to the right, down the path, like that was where he had intended to go anyway and he had only been playing his own kind of trick on me and making me waste my ammunition. It was a trick only a fool would have been impressed by, and I gave myself credit for the second round.

I sat on the branch again and watched the bass breaking water. A couple of fish even bigger than mine swam in the shallows almost under the tree's furthest tip. I watched them trolling for flies and mosquitoes, and I thought of throwing them a couple of Tom Brown's Beetles. But I didn't think anything that light would reach the water, and watching the river ripple made me realize again how thirsty I was. I was getting cotton mouth and my throat was getting cakey. But the dogs were too close in to go for a drink.

As if they knew what I was thinking, the lead dog circled around and out of the woods and led them over to the stream to drink. That made me mad, and I got up and fired off a log uselessly and cursed them until my throat got too dry to curse them any more. Then I sat down again and thought about being hungry to keep from thinking about being thirsty until I finally got interested in a Yellow-Tufted Chickadee at the end of the long branch that went out almost over the river.

When he left, I watched two sparrows have an aerial battle that covered the length of what I could see of the river branch and beyond. They moved as if someone had tied their feet together and threw them into the air. Yoked by their motion, they rolled around some invisible center at the speed of sound. The sheer grace of it took me on into the afternoon, and the clouds told me how much longer I would have to wait.

About an hour before sunset, the sparrows came back and did it all again, only lower over the water this time. I developed the idea that their territories overlapped and they always fought after a day of hunting. But the longer I watched them, the more it seemed that they worked in tandem like two fishermen with a seine net taking the insects that had moved down closer to the water with the setting sun. The first time I thought about being thirsty after that was when the first drops of rain hit me, about an hour after dark.

I caught what I could in my mouth, and what I could scrape off the trunk and branches, but it wasn't a heavy or a steady rain and what I got was only enough to buy me a little time. It cooled off again after the rain, and the branches were damp and uncomfortable. The clouds were cutting the visibility way down and I knew that I was going to feel thirsty again if I didn't find something to do; so I decided to build a fire. It occurred to me that no one I had ever heard of had built a fire in an open tree, and it seemed like a worthwhile challenge. If I kept it small, the risks would be minimal.

I went all over the tree getting my assortment of twigs. I decided that the first fire ever built in a tree ought to be a ceremonial fire at least, and that deserved no less than a shading of twigs and tinder that approached an art form. I spent a couple of hours going up and down on the slippery branches gathering just the right sticks.

I made a platform in the fork of a branch level with the ground and stacked all my materials on it. Then I built a nest of smaller and finer teepees with the kindling and reached for my wallet and two strikable matches. I wondered if maybe I could make some torches and drive the dogs off with them. The second time through every pocket, I realized that my wallet and my matches were down in the pack the dogs had fought over before I had started shelling them.

It was too dark to see exactly where they were at the bottom of the tree, or even if they were there at all. But I wanted the matches, so I went down. Fortunately, one of them scented me on the lowest branch and woke up with a growl and a blind leap that didn't even come close but sent me back up the tree until daybreak.

I was not really hungry, or at least not hungry enough to starting eating my own species of beetle, but I knew that when I did get hungry enough, there was a whole tree full of ants. The hunger took care of itself, at least long enough for me to strap myself in for a little sleep, so I'd be alert when the dogs nodded off again. It was late afternoon when I woke up.

I looked around for the dogs at the bottom of the tree but they were gone. For a minute I was elated, but then I thought of the humiliation of having been treed like some greenhorn hunter and I wished they were back again so that I could redeem myself and even the score. I was cursing them for cowards when I raised my eyes and saw them again back across the log and up on the little rise where I had first seen them.

They were coaxing me down, no doubt. But there was more to it than that. The Alpha dog was missing. I swung myself as far around the tree as I could to see if he was waiting in ambush under the tree or in the grass, but he wasn't there. Then I got down as far as I could in the tree and tried to see what I could of the tracks.

The lead dog's tracks were easy to pick out even from the tree, and I followed them only by their size to the log bridge. On the far side, the prints curved back and were lost in the main body of prints. It was too far away to be sure. I thought that perhaps he was on the far side of the log laughing at me again. But I felt that he was closer than that for some reason. There was no way to check the underbrush inland, so I decided to take a calculated risk. If he came bounding through the underbrush, I could beat him back to the tree easily. The path into the woods was clear far enough that he couldn't be hiding along it within catching distance. I decided to go down.

I was halfway to the pack when I realized it was a mistake. The Alpha dog came bounding out of the grass on the far side of the log and started to cross it. But those minutes in the current were still with him, and they slowed him over the log long enough for me to get to the tree and start shinning up it.

He was not slow once he hit dry land though, and I grabbed for that branch and yanked myself up as he left the ground. Luckily, he was a little off to the side, and I saw his teeth go by my thigh halfway down his muzzle before I pulled my legs up entirely. He fell back as I threw one leg up over the limb. If I had let it dangle down the other side, he would have torn me down, stripping the muscles of my leg like stockings.

I held my feet up in the air behind and above as I lay on the branch to strike downward as he came flying upward. I pulled my thickest stick out of the back of my jeans and slammed it down at him. He caught the stick in his teeth, clamping onto it and jerking it out of my hand as he fell back down. I yanked my arm back and went up the rest of the tree like it was a ladder, until I sat at the top-most sittable branch listening to my heart thump.

The dog was barking his victory or his anger at just missing me. Either way, it was an insult I couldn't ignore, and I climbed back down the tree almost as fast as I had come up. I yanked one of the thick branches out of my fire platform and threw it down at him.

The fire platform capsized and went down between the branches. My stick missed the Alpha dog, but the rest of the platform fell almost on top of him and sent him yelping back. I laughed so hard I almost fell out of the tree, and he bounded to the bottom of it to get me when I fell. But I caught another branch and let a leg dangle just enough to make a leap at it look a little less than ridiculous. The dog leaped.

I danced around from branch to branch, pretending to fall every once in a while until he stopped going for it and went off muttering across the log. Before he went across, he looked back at me and then at the log again, and I knew that the next time I came down, he was going to come across it a lot faster than he had this time.

I watched the sun go down again and felt the temperature drop out of spring and almost back into winter. The wind picked up for a while after dark, and I strapped myself in for the night. But my sleep was bad, and my dreams were full of the faces of dogs snarling into mine.

Toward morning I had a dream about Indians dropping out of the trees onto canoe parties, and it stayed with me after I woke up. I didn't know why until almost noon, but it made me feel very relaxed and confident. The dogs had come back across the log, but I pelted them with a few sticks while I was thinking, and they went back across the log, pretending to hurry as if I had driven them off. But their act wouldn't have fooled a squirrel.

I made a long throw after them that made me lean out too far, and I dropped straight down the trunk to the next branch. I grabbed the branch I had just been standing on and caught myself before I fell all the way, but it made my heart race. My stick sailed out over the bank and into the river. One of the dogs stopped to watch it land and caused a traffic jam that had the last dog's hind leg clawing the side of the log for a foothold. The fight started on the log and carried on over onto the far bank, and before it was finished, I knew how I was going to get away.

The day had warmed considerably by the time I made my move. I waited for them to nap in the sun, but I waited too long. Those that dozed seemed to do it in shifts, and the Alpha dog never even pretended to close his eyes. Just before I gave up on them, they gave up on me and started for the log. If they came across before I got down, I would be stuck in the tree for another day and night. The Alpha dog was in the middle of the log when I hit the ground. The fall was harder than I expected, but I bounced toward the stream and scrambled across a little space of land and into the water.

The stream had been the key to it all along, but it had taken a dream to tell me what I should have known after the Alpha dog went yelping down the current. They were afraid of fast moving water, they would never go into it by choice. There were no canoe parties for me to drop on out of my tree, but my dream was right. The dogs came right up to the water, but they wouldn't come in.

I hung just offshore on an exposed root of the tree, and they leaned down to snap at me trying to reach me without falling in. I hoped they wouldn't, although the odds were in favor of my drowning any of them that did. Those faces snapping so close to mine were the faces of my dream, and I knew that I was where I was supposed to be. But I had a long way to go, and there were plenty of places along the way where the Alpha dog would get his chance.

I pushed off the root and let the current carry me to a tree limb that was hung up toward the middle of the stream. I rested there for a moment and gulped in some more water, but not too much. The water was cold, and the river branch wound seven or eight miles before it came into the main river and out near the bus station at Toms River. It was a long way to go and I pushed off.

There were dogs on both sides of the bank by then. The Beta dog and two others had gone around by way of the log and barked along after me from the far bank. The Alpha dog and two smaller ones took the near bank as far as they could. I weighed the odds. Already out of the water and armed with a strong stick, I had a better than even chance of driving off the Beta dog and his pack. But coming up the bank wet and slippery with mud into those teeth did not seem like a good bet. Properly armed, I could have killed the Alpha dog and driven off the rest, but without at least a knife, it was not a match I wanted, and I stayed to the middle of the stream.

The bank was uneven in a lot of places and the dogs had to go inland. When I was lucky, the bank clogged where I had to go through slow water so they were not there to dive in after me. There was one place where I could have come ashore as the path along the bank shot almost directly inland, but the other three dogs were close on the far bank, and their barking would have drawn the Alpha dog to my trail almost immediately. At best, I would be treed in a worse place than before. I took the sluggish current and swam with it further downstream.

At the second slow place I wasn't so lucky. The river branch rushed into a stony bottomed shallows and all but died. For fifty yards or so it was a lake. The dogs came down on both sides and fanned out waiting for me to come to the middle of their gauntlet so they could roll up its ends on me. When I stood up, the water was just a little over my waist, and a few feet away it was even shallower.

The Alpha dog waited in the middle, opposite the Beta dog. He looked as if he was going to get even and he was going to make it long and painful. It was one of the greatest pleasures of my life up to that time when I beaned him on the head with a river stone the size of an egg. The others looked at him, and one after the other I hit them in the back, the side, on the foot.

All those days chucking stones in the summer down in the desert and skipping them out across the river had paid off. I had six hits on the first seven stones, and every dog was hit twice before it got over the first hit. They went howling off into the woods out of range. I stuck stones in every pocket and carried as many as I could in my hands.

I started down through the deepest part of the trough, cursing them and challenging them to come out. In the middle, the water was at mid-thigh, and the Alpha dog made his move. But the others followed him reluctantly, and after I had hit him twice, once on the paw, the others turned and ran, and he limped off behind them. The Beta dog left the woods late and turned back as soon as I threw the first rock in his direction.

The stream got deeper again and narrowed, and I walked slowly down there challenging them to come out. But none of them came, and I flung the last of my rocks and dove into the stream where it picked up speed again. It took them almost half a mile to catch up with me, but there was no easy place to come ashore, and no place where I would have the advantages I had in the river. But a little way further down I almost had to rethink my decision.

Up ahead, branches and debris had formed a log jam that narrowed the flow of the river to a deep trench that two dogs leaning across could cover almost entirely. All the way down, I had been watching for low hanging branches where the Alpha dog might come out over the water and take a bite as I went past. I was at such a place and the dogs knew it. All six of them ran ahead and waited. I paddled out of the main current and grabbed an overhanging branch that stuck out of the bank.

There was another branch I could pull myself part way up the bank with, and I tested it by hanging on while I figured out how to get the dogs away from the spillway between the jammed up branches. I moved down along the bank mostly in the water until I got about ten yards down from the upstream branch. Then I grabbed a branch along the bank and heaved one of my last rocks at the Alpha dog.

I hit one of the smaller dogs instead, but it was a loss of prestige for him anyway, and he came snarling and snapping up the path until all three dogs were leaning out over the bank above me, snarling and making little lunges into the air. I took a deep breath and pushed myself down under the water and swam as hard as I could upstream staying close to the bank where the current was weakest. The dogs ran down toward the log jam and were almost there when I surfaced at the upstream branch.

"You idiots!" I shouted at them, "I'm up *here*!" Gradually, after I cursed them and their immediate lineage, they ran back up the bank and I pretended to be climbing up to meet them. When they were almost above me, I went down under the water and shoved off. I held my breath as long as I could, but I had to break surface just short of the spillway. When I did, they were all still upstream barking at the water.

If I had any sense, of course, I wouldn't have looked back. The sight of the dogs snarling and snapping at an empty stream was too much for me, and I started laughing. Water splashed into my open mouth as I went over the little spillway. I started to choke, but the current zipped me along. The dogs had started running again the minute they heard my laughter, and I made up less ground on them than I would have otherwise.

But the river was swift and ten feet wide again; the only thing they could do was run along the bank growling and barking and biting the air. I lay back and relaxed. It almost cost me dearly. A little way ahead, there was a rock that jutted up through the water close to shore. The Alpha dog had leaped out onto it and crouched there waiting for me to pass, drifting close to the shore without noticing it.

At the last moment, I looked up and saw that face leering down at me. I threw my feet up and hit the rock with them, jerking myself toward the bank. The current countered my motion exactly and held me straight. I pulled the last rock from my pocket and threw it.

He was too close to miss, but I missed him. He lunged, his huge Doberman jaws gnashing the air. But the lunge put him on the slippery part of the rock and he fell off. I thought I was going to have to fight him there in the water, and I tried to cling to the rock and climb out.

It was too slippery. I waited for him to come paddling around the rock, but he didn't, and eventually I came around the rock myself. But he wasn't there waiting. Fifty yards downstream, he was working his way up a steep bank with his hind feet still in the water. I kicked out into the current, ashamed of my carelessness. I stayed alert the rest of the trip, and when the river narrowed and slowed at the same point, I swam over to the bank and broke off the longest, straightest branches I could.

I had no knife, so I rubbed them on the stones to sharpen them. The points were not good, but they were all I had. The best possible biting place was only wide enough for one dog at a time on each side, and the Alpha and Beta dogs got the positions. I took the Beta dog first, coming close to his bank and slashing at him with the thinnest of the branches like a whip. Eventually, I hit him in the eye, and he backed off shaking his head and blinking.

I took the Alpha dog on the point. It wasn't much, but a short, sharp thrust was enough to draw blood, and a good shot might get an eye or something equally valuable. He snapped at the stick and caught it in his teeth. He tugged, I pulled. He tugged harder and planted his front feet. I lunged with the second sharpest stick. He yelped and jumped back. There was a little blood on the end of the stick. I swam for it the rest of the way and got past before the other dogs could get into striking position.

The rest of the trip as far as the Parkway was so dull I doubled back upstream on them. I got out and hit one of the Beta dogs with a stone and let them chase me back in. One other time they got close, but it was only on the Beta bank, and I held them back until I got past with the full branch of a tree I had pulled out of the river further up.

The Beta dog was keeping one eye closed most of the time, and I managed to pull a boulder loose from the bank in one place and hit one of the Alpha dogs in the ribs so hard that he gradually fell behind and eventually dropped out. But I started to get uncomfortable from the cold water a mile or so above the Parkway bridge. I thought that they would not cross the road, and that they would abandon the chase when I went under the bridge and turn back. I pulled myself part way up onto one of the concrete drain pipes and dried off a bit.

But there was a cold wind blowing by then, and the afternoon was cooling way down, and I was better off in the water. When I floated out on the other side of the bridge, they were on the banks waiting for me. It looked like I was going to have to go all the way to the bus station, and I didn't like it.

The Alpha dog kept running along the bank with his one follower, and the Beta dog kept up on the other side just to keep me in the water. They were too far away to have a shot at me then, and when the river emptied into the main branch, they would have no chance at all. But they pursued me anyway, and I resented it.

I resented having to stay in the water, and I resented what they did to my food and my pack and the fact that they had treed me to begin with. But not letting me out, hanging on like that when it was clear that I'd won, was plain bad sportsmanship. I shook my fist at the Alpha dog as the river carried me on my back and called him every name I could think of. All the rest of the way, I shouted at him all the ways I was going to make life short and miserable for him when I finally caught up with him again.

Finally, the river widened out and the Beta dogs gave up. The branch deposited me in a side eddy, and I swam the rest of the way to my left toward the bus station. I pulled myself out onto the beach and lay there for a minute, wet, chilled, and tired. When I picked myself up and looked back across the mouth of the river branch, I could see the Alpha dog standing on the furthest spit of land leaning forward out over the water as if some wind might blow me back within jaws' reach.

It was too far away to be sure, but I thought I saw his tongue lolling out as if he were laughing at me. It didn't matter. We were far from even, but we both knew I'd won. I looked at him gnawing the air so far away across the impassable gulf, and I laughed a great exuberant laugh that went out across the water like an almost final insult. Then I gave him the finger and hurried on up the bank.

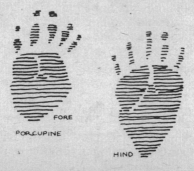

FORE

PORCUPINE

HIND

SKUNK IN MUD

8/Omen

I was tired, wet, and getting cold as I walked to Rick's house from the river. I was proud that I had escaped, but there was no question in my mind that nothing had been accomplished unless I went back to my camp and refused to be driven off it again. All animals have a territory they will defend. I had mine, and I still have it. Unless I went back and defended it, the Pine Barrens would belong to the dogs by default. Even though I had outsmarted and tormented them, I had left the territory. Unless I wanted to fight them off every time I went into the woods, I would have to reestablish my right to be there.

I dried off and ate at Rick's house. Hot chocolate warmed me, and the food filled me more easily than I expected. I told Rick about the dogs and convinced him that our right to go into the woods was being challenged and that unless we met the challenge immediately, we would have to spend most of our time in the woods fighting off the dogs.

He agreed and we assembled the baseball bats, and our machetes, and our knives. Stalking Wolf came in while my clothes were drying. "You look like a man who has just outsmarted something," he said. I told him the whole story of the dogs and he nodded when I had finished. "So you outsmarted the Guardians." He pursed his lips. "Perhaps you will become someone very special after all." The word that he used was not "special," but an Indian word he said had no direct translation.

I asked him if he thought that we must go back and reestablish ourselves and he nodded. "Even if there is no one else there you must go," he said, and he was right. Unless I went back immediately, the shadow of those dogs would play across my mind all the time I was in the woods. To be free in the woods, you must be free in yourself. I put on my clothes and Rick and I started out the door. "Watch for the omens," he said. I nodded and Rick and I began the hike back to my camp.

All the way, we prepared to fight the last great battle for the Pines, the Dog Wars. We hefted our bats and had Tom Sawyer fantasies of ourselves back to back in the middle of the Alpha pack, making them pay dearly for our lives. But when we got there, the dogs had gone, and my pack wasn't as badly torn up as I had expected. We made our camp and waited, but everything semed so different looking at it from the ground that if I hadn't camped there so often before, I would have sworn it was a different place. Even the stars seemed to have changed, and the tree seemed to have been subtly altered, although I could not say how.

When the sun went down, it did not have the glory it had had above the trees, and the banks of the river branch did not darken with the same complexity. Once during the night we heard the bay of the dogs way up beyond Stoney Hill, but no dogs came near us that night nor the next day. We went back home disappointed that our great battle had not come off, but satisfied that the dogs knew we were there and intended to stay.

When we got back to Rick's, Stalking Wolf asked me if I had encountered any exceptionally powerful medicine. I told him that the place was "different" but I could not say how. He looked at me as if he expected more, but when it was clear that there was nothing more to say, he nodded and turned back to what he was doing without saying anything else.

We remained ready for a confrontation with the dogs for a week, but we did not run into them again. Satisfied that they were either avoiding us or preoccupied elsewhere, we planned a fossil-collecting expedition to a dump a few miles up from the Good Medicine Cabin. The dump had four big, square pits like open-topped rooms in which the fourth wall was a ramp the bulldozer had backed up and down to dig out the rest. Three of the pits had been filled in with garbage and covered over, but the fourth had been abandoned empty, and we expected that its walls, running thirty feet into the earth, would be full of fossils and other interesting things.

The birds that frequented the dump would make the trip worthwhile even if there was nothing to be found in the abandoned pit. We had a patrol meeting Friday night so we did not get to the campsite until after dark. We made a short trip to the dump, but even with a moon, the pit was dark as an open grave and the ragged mounds of dirt along the rim looked like the teeth of some enormous dog.

It looked better in the daylight and we were down in it early in the morning. The ramp had eroded and a wide section of it near the top had fallen in on itself leaving a drop-off of about eight feet deep before the ramp began again. We jumped down it easily into the soft dirt, and began to explore.

From the bottom of the pit, the piles along the rim towered fifty feet above us. The walls were almost vertical, but the end wall had clefts and niches where the bulldozer had taken its uneven bites. There were dog tracks around the pit, but they were a day old, and we had seen the dogs taking one of their runs down toward Blanchard's and we were sure they would not be back until nightfall, if then.

The fossils, however, did not materialize, and what had looked like it might be a deer carcass from the rim turned out to be an oddly folded tarpaulin. Still, the way the clouds marched over the peaks of dirt at the top of the pit was fascinating, and we sat and watched them intermittently for most of the morning.

Somewhere toward noon, we got the idea of climbing the rear wall of the pit by digging handholds into the soft but well-packed earth and using the natural ledges and niches to rest in. There was a small dirt ledge and a crevice about three feet wide a third of the way up the wall. The wall went almost vertically most of the way, although the top five or ten feet slanted back as if it had been dug out from above to keep the trucks from backing over the edge.

We were a handhold short of reaching the ledge when we saw the dogs. At first I thought I saw a flash of shadow disappear down one of the mounds, but I told myself that it couldn't be what I thought it was. When the dogs appeared at the top of the ramp there was no doubt. I counted fifteen of them appearing and disappearing over the lip of the pit until they were all gathered at the far end, satisfied that we were indeed trapped and easy game.

They hesitated for a while at the drop-off, and I dug the last handhold like a terrier. I pulled myself up into the niche and reached down for Rick just as the last of the dogs jumped down into the pit.

The first of the dogs made it to the foot of the cliff just a little too late to make a leap for Rick as I grabbed his arm and pulled him up. There was barely room for both of us on the ledge, and I turned and started to dig handholds in the wall above us. Below us, the dogs barked and leapt uselessly up the wall.

The wall of the pit was made of soft but well-packed clay and sand. Normally the handhold would only be as deep as our wrists, but the face was so sheer and the quality of the soil so unpredictable that I dug into the wall to arm's length. By reaching well into them and grabbing a handful of dirt to make my fist too wide to pop back out, I managed to pull myself up to where I could dig the next handhold. Handholds became footholds as I dug new handholds further up, and in half an hour or so, I was more than halfway up the cliff, digging as I went. Rick sat on the ledge waiting for me to get to the top so he could come up after me without both of us falling if one of my handholds caved it.

The dogs had stopped barking and were milling around or sitting with their heads cocked watching my climb. When it dawned on them where I was going, six of them turned and bolted for thc ramp. The rest started leaping up toward the ledge again. Rick was still out of their reach, but in falling back, two of the dogs started a landslide in the lower wall and part of the ledge went with it. With this new base to spring from, their leaps were coming almost up to the ledge, and I turned back to my digging with a kind of frenzy.

I knew that the dogs were going to get to the top before I did, but when I looked back over my shoulder to see where they were, I saw them sniffing around the drop-off of the ramp or trying without success to leap and scramble up it. I shouted down to Rick that they were trapped, and he shouted back up that more of the ledge was crumbling. I turned back to my digging.

The handholds were good, but as had happened so many times when we had climbed a dirt cliff this way, they crumbled under the pressure of a shoe. My arms could reach way in and hold, but my feet went in only partway and broke the dirt away no matter how carefully I pulled them out. It was going to be an even harder climb for Rick. He sat below and threw stones down at the dogs, but another foot of ledge crumbled as he did and he almost fell. When I looked down, he was wedged back into the niche with his fingers dug into the walls.

The dirt got looser the further up I got, and the handholds weaker, and I knew that the last of them would not hold Rick. I had to reach in all the way to my arm pit and dig my fingers into the soil to pull myself up. At the point where the sheer wall slanted back away from the pit, one of the footholds crumbled completely and left my foot dangling, while I squeezed my handfuls of dirt to keep my hands from pulling out of the holes.

I flared my elbows to wedge my arms in, but kick as I might, I could not reestablish the foothold. Slowly, I took out my right hand and dug a shallow hold near my waist. I pulled my knee up and wedged it into the foothold and reached up and dug another handhold and pulled myself up.

The dogs had given up trying to get out and had returned to take out their frustration by barking and leaping up at Rick. Every once in a while, one of the dogs would dig its claws into the bank as it fell back and cause more landsliding. I dug one more crumbling handhold and pulled myself up the last of the slope.

At the top, I shouted down to Rick that I was going back to camp for the rope and the clubs. The dogs were barking and running back and forth along the rear wall of the pit, and I ran along the top of the dirt piles hoping to draw them away from Rick. About ten of them ran along the inside of the pit following me, and about eight of those stayed at the break in the ramp, barking at it and trying to climb back out.

I ran all the way to the camp and back, the rope coiled over my shoulder. When I got to the edge of the pit, the dogs were all back at the rear wall, but they were lying down, or barking halfheartedly at Rick. One of them was on the top of the landslide with his front feet up the wall, barking. I threw the rope over the side and called to Rick to climb up, but the rope was too short and he had to come up through the crumbling handholds on the sheer face of the pit to reach it.

Pushing off crumbled the last of the ledge, and Rick was left with no way to go but up. He climbed slowly. Because I was bigger, the handholds were a little too far apart for him and a little too deep, and the climbing was difficult. The handholds deteriorated the further up he got, and he had to dig new ones near mine to make the last ten feet to where the rope dangled about five feet down the sheer part of the wall. When he was almost level with it, first one foothold went and then the other, and he had to throw himself off the face of the cliff and grab for the rope.

The jolt almost pulled me over the lip of the slope. In my haste to get the rope down to him, I had forgotten to tie it to anything, and I had to take the full weight of his climb. I had the rope up one arm, over my shoulder, and down to the other hand. And when I leaned back and dug my heels in, I could support Rick's weight. But because I had not realized how hard that was going to be, I was standing too close to the edge and Rick's leap almost pulled me over.

The dogs were up and barking, and some of them were jumping uselessly up against the wall a good twenty feet below Rick. I screamed to him to hurry up but he was muddy and slippery, and the faster he climbed, the more inevitably I was being pulled over the cliff. I was partway down the gentlest part of the slope as he came over the lip where the wall sloped back, and I lay back so I was almost touching the ground to hold his weight. Rick scrambled up the rope and over me, then turned and pulled me up to the top again with his hand.

We sat a long time on the dirt piles catching our breath and looking down at the dogs who were now at our mercy as I had been at theirs when I was in the tree. Some of them seemed to sense that and threw themselves into a frenzied attack on the drop-off of the ramp. But none of them were even close to getting out. They were trapped; they knew it, and we knew it.

I sat looking at them and what came to mind was not the dogs as they had been along the river, but that face of fangs that had come leaping at me out of the bushes years before. The terror had long since turned to smouldering anger, and I looked down at the dogs with a hatred and rage I had never let myself feel before. The dogs were now *my* victims and Rick and I scoured the dumps for the biggest and heaviest objects we could find. It took us more than an hour to drag the pieces of log and cinderblock to the edge of the pit. The dogs milled below barking and growling.

All the fear I had for Rick while I was running back to camp, and all the fear that came to the surface only in dreams, welled up in me, and I lifted a huge log above my head and stood looking down at the dogs. I hated them at that moment in a way I could not understand then, though I have come now to realize that hate is just fear worn inside out, and it was my fear, and not my hatred, that drove me.

I lifted the log and thought of how the dogs would have leapt on us if we had tumbled down among them. I thought of those fangs tearing at my face. I thought of what it would have been like lying half stunned, kicking at them only by reflex while they tore at us. I heaved the log with all my strength.

It fell in the middle of the dogs with such force that it stuck in the ground. But it did not hit any of them. I turned to pick up another. Rick stood holding neither a log nor a stone. I looked at him for a moment, and I knew what he was thinking because I had thought it myself. The dogs were trapped, they had no chance. It did not seem right to slaughter them like that. But all those times when I bent to pick up something near the side of a trail and that ghost dog leapt snarling at my face driving the joy of my find away in a rush of fear and trembling, urged me to throw another. I picked up a piece of cinderblock and went back to the edge. Rick said nothing. I lifted it and picked a dog. There would be no random miss this time.

But as I lifted the cinderblock, the dog looked up at me with his head cocked and the anger drained out of me. He looked not like a wild dog but like my own dog. I let the cinder block drop and turned away. I looked at Rick and he shrugged. "Grandfather says they're the Guardians," he said. It was true. If it had not been for the dogs, there would have been campers everywhere we turned, filling our forest with beer cans, slaughtering the trees, butchering the animals. When I looked back down at the dogs I saw them in a new way, not as enemies but as adversaries, doing their job in the pattern of things, opposing us with no more malice than an owl has for a rabbit. There was no killing them after that. But there was no leaving them there either. "I suppose we have to get them out," I said. Rick was already carrying two cinder blocks toward the ramp.

We threw the logs and rocks and cinder blocks down into a pile at the base of the drop-off, but it still left the dogs too far down to scramble out. It was hot, sweaty work, and Rick went back to bring back some food while I scoured the dump for some other way to get them out. We sat on the dirt pile and ate our lunch. Rick tossed a piece of his sandwich down among them and before long the whole pack was milling around under us wagging their tails and barking for food.

I believe that was the first time I realized how really hungry some of them were. A few, the ones who had come to beg first, were still on the border of well fed, but the others were lean almost to scrawniness. We threw them the rest of our lunch and went back to camp for more. The longer we fed them, the more they looked like ordinary dogs and the more we felt sorry for their being trapped in there.

We spent the next hour looking for something they could run out on, and finally we found an old refrigerator that we thought would do the trick. We pushed and slid, and hauled it until we had it right at the edge of the drop-off of the ramp. The dogs charged up the ramp toward us and suddenly they didn't look as cute as they had before. They looked like creatures that lived harsh lives under implacable rules of survival and had been changed by it in a way that could not be reversed by a few crumbs. When they began to bark, they were no longer my dog or Rick's but the Guardians, and any four of them would have been more than a match for us, even armed. "You know what's going to happen if we push this thing in," I said to Rick. He looked at the dogs as if he was seeing them in a new way too and he said, "Yeah, we're going to be standing around in the middle of fifteen wild dogs who didn't have enough lunch."

Rick went back over and got the rope, and I pounded a stake in the ground. We tied the rope to the refrigerator and lowered it so that it teetered over the lip of the drop-off. Then we built a teepee of sticks under the rope and Rick went back to camp and got one of our candles. We lit the candle, put it in the middle of the tinder and ran. Fifteen minutes later we were still waiting for the fire to flare up and burn through the rope. There was a little puff of smoke as the flame hit the tinder, and then nothing. The rope still held. We drew straws to see who would go, by plucking grass. I never had the knack for it, and mine broke off about an inch beyond my fingers while Rick snapped his own at the base. I took the machete and walked back across the dump.

All the way back, I tried to convince myself that maybe the refrigerator wouldn't work after all, or that maybe it would take them a while to figure it out. But when I cut that rope, I knew they would be up and over the lip of the ramp before I went ten steps, and I was right. I slashed the rope and ran faster than I should have been able to toward the trees. I could hear the barking closer and closer, but I knew if I looked back, I'd stumble and that would be it.

The dogs sounded as if they were right on top of me when I noticed that they were running along with me. I thought at first that they were either toying with me or trying to surround me on the run and force me to stop. I was so surprised that they hadn't attacked me, that I stopped running and drew the machete. But the dogs stopped when I stopped, and pranced around wagging their tails. I couldn't believe it. They trotted around nice as house dogs.

After Rick came out of the trees, they came back to camp with us, and we gave them some more food. They sprawled around or played and one or two came over to be petted. When we went to sleep, they lay down around our camp fire and went to sleep with us. But when we woke up, they were gone, and the camp seemed empty, as if they had never been there.

It seemed to us that they were truly spirit dogs and had vanished with the sun. But whether they were live dogs or not, they were certainly not ordinary dogs, and to us they were *very* good medicine.

About a year later, Rick and I were crossing a field and we saw a pack of dogs come in on the shortest side of it. They were a lot closer to us than to the camper who was repacking his car along the road, and they came running toward us, disappearing and reappearing in the grass as they ran. Their barking and snarling had a tone to it I had heard too often before. It was the cry of a pack of dogs that has found something it thinks it can kill with ease.

There is a certain pitch to it that terrifies hunters when they hear it in the woods, and it differs from all other cries a pack of dogs can make. When I spent the summer studying the Alpha pack, the largest wild dog pack in the Pine Barrens, I learned to tell from the tone of their cry what kind of game they were on to and what risk of death or injury. And even years after I could pick that cry from any other because it raised memories in the blood that have nothing to do with rationality.

Their cry made us look for either a good tree or some sort of weapon, but at the same time we didn't move toward either. We just stood there watching them come. There was a smooth natural beauty to the way they moved that seemed as marvelous as anything I had seen in the woods. The way their leaps carried them over and into the grass seemed to have a perfection to it that was beautiful.

I crouched down so that I could see them breaking over the top of the grass at eye level, and they looked like they were flowing up and over the water like the dolphins I had seen once surfing, with the ocean eyelevel off the end of my board. I saw for a moment, not the dogs, but their motion and I saw that their attack was as beautiful as their friendship. I stood up and watched them come without knowing what I would do when they came except that, whatever I did, it would move in the same great design as their motion moved in. When they were halfway to us, I began to recognize individual dogs, and I waited for them to recognize me. When they were about fifty yards away I began to wonder how much hunger dulls the memory and whether they had the same memory of things I had.

But a stride or two closer, and the siren of their cry wound down as they veered off and swung in a wide arc back toward the camper. He threw down his gear and dove for the car, squirming around like a mouse in a bottle trying to get all the windows shut. The Beta dog got to the wrong door as he was winding up the last one, and the man must have sprung back into the driver's seat half an inch from the teeth on the other side of the glass. Two got up on his hood and barked at him through the window with their front legs stiff and bent back so he could get the full effect of their fangs.

The rest of the dogs went through his gear and shredded everything that could be shredded looking for food. He started the car eventually and screeched out onto the road on two wheels. The dogs scrambled off as soon as it began to move, but he went swerving up the road anyway as if he had planned to shake the dogs off that way, and liked the idea so much that he did it, watching imaginary dogs fly off the hood.

I stood waiting for them to finish with the camp and come running back. There was a moment, when the dogs had run beside me more than a year before, when I had had to risk stopping. It was a wonderful and terrible moment, and I waited for it to happen again. But one by one, they took what they could and ran to the woods at the far end of the field, without looking at us and without looking back. I had the oddest feeling as they went past that what had passed between us had been a military courtesy between neutrals who might some day have to kill each other.

It may well have been that when we ran into them the first time they were a newly formed pack, made up of a few stragglers who couldn't keep up with the bigger pack and a number of dogs newly gone wild who had surrendered to us on the principles of some canine logic. It may have been that they were totally wild now and stayed away from us only from some dim memory of having once been defeated by us. But that does not explain why they did not look at us, as they might have been expected to when passing something dangerous.

In either case they were, both times, an omen. An omen is nature favoring us with a remarkable event, the glow from which makes our life different for a while. The fact that a mechanical explanation can be found does not mean it's the only one, nor does it cease to be the work of some larger and more encompassing form simply because the tools it uses can be understood. The dogs were to me a sign of the passing of some larger force, some more complex pattern, something within my perception but beyond my complete understanding. They were an omen, a mark of continuing grandeur beyond explanation.

When Stalking Wolf said that a thing was an omen he did not mean that it predicted the coming of some event. An omen is an experience that interprets all events that follow it and reinterprets everything that went before. Good medicine, bad medicine, and omens change our understanding of our relationship to the world. Nothing is ever exactly the same once you have experienced an omen.

When I went to see the beauty of the dogs, I felt the tranquility of opening to nature completely, without restraint. Years later, I was to learn its violence.

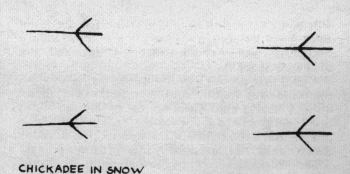

CHICKADEE IN SNOW

9/Chickadee Survival

Of all the birds, Stalking Wolf respected the chickadee the most, even more than the hawk or the owl. Every animal had some characteristic to admire and emulate, and Stalking Wolf often used them as examples of what our own skills should be like. We learned to be patient observers like the owl. We learned cleverness from the crow, and courage from the jay, who will attack an owl ten times its size to drive it off its territory. But above all of them ranked the chickadee because of its indomitable spirit.

The exuberance of the chickadee made him our idol. In the coldest weather, when other birds have gone into the brush to wait behind a dome of driven snow for the weather to clear, the chickadee is always out, his *chickadee-dee-dee* ringing off the snow. When the fox has curled himself up under a small tree and let the snow drift him a blanket of insulation, the chickadee is out doing loop-the-loops over the seedless snow, calling louder than playing children that he is there and alive and happy about it!

A chickadee doesn't look like a good bet for survival; you could close your hand with one in the palm almost without hurting him. There are better fliers; swallows have more grace and all the soaring birds are more spectacular. But nobody flies with more reckless abandon than the chickadee, and nobody flies with more delight.

The chickadee lives by joyous faith in living. Whenever everything else curls up and prepares to wait, or die, the chickadee is out in the middle of it. I have heard them even in the middle of a blizzard, chirping with that dancing tone over and over into the cold air, as if it thinks that hiding from a storm is the craziest form of self-denial.

His voice comes out of the cold silence like the last voice in the world, singing that everything which has gone under the snow is neither lost nor dead and that life survives beautifully somewhere else and will return. There is a joy in its song that says that everybody who is hiding from the storm is missing the best part. Rick and I thought so too. We loved storms.

We used to sit out on the beach and watch them from down the coast, rolling back in over the land after they has passed once to the southwest. The storms were different with the season; winter lightning was different from summer lightning, even the color of the clouds was different. Ice went to the top of the sky in summer but it hung low in the heavy march of snow clouds in January and February, turning sunsets pink and purple.

The wind moved in a different way from season to season and brought the storms in at different angles. When we saw a square cliff of clouds dragging its own darkness behind it, we settled down with the animals and started tucking ourselves into the woods to watch the storm come in. Even during the worst of it, except for being wet and sometimes cold, we were happier than we could have been at home, inside a house built to keep everything out.

We were never afraid of storms. They changed the world, made everything we had seen into something else. The windstorm and the northeaster changed the patterns of the branches, made alterations in the canopy. The snowstorm rounded everything into subtle curves, freezing in time the motion of each tree, each branch.

The concept of being "safe from the storm" never made any sense to us; the storm was beautiful. Nature could not harm us if we were part of it, if we trusted it and were one with it. We were out in the most outrageous conditions without mishap because it never occurred to us that things could be otherwise. Animals, with far fewer resources than we had, managed to live through storms, so we saw no reason why we shouldn't. With Stalking Wolf's help we were as adapted to the cold as the animals and we had learned to survive without difficulty.

Not everyone understood that, least of all the two scoutmasters who led the troop we had joined on its first winter campout. We learned in less than a year that the scouts did not have much to teach us about nature or survival that Stalking Wolf or the *Boy Scout Handbook* had not already taught us. Still, being scouts gave us a chance to get into new woods to the south, and the campout in December was a fantastic opportunity. We were up and out in the woods hours before the early risers. We hadn't been scouts very long, and we had no regard for the discipline necessary to keep twenty-five kids from getting lost, killed, or injured. We didn't need anyone to protect us from the woods; the idea was as crazy as hiding from storms. So we got up early and went wherever there might be something of interest.

We knew the storm was coming hours before anyone else did, and we knew that it was going to be a great one to watch. When it started to gather at the western edge of the sky, we started to look around for a place to weather the storm and watch it. But we knew we'd be in trouble if we did. Our parents had warned us repeatedly about wandering off and making everybody worry about us, and we decided to go back nearer to camp. We consoled ourselves with the idea that perhaps one of the scoutmasters might know something about storms that we didn't.

The scoutmaster was a well-meaning man, but even when he stood up he seemed to be sitting behind a desk. It did not seem likely that he would know something about the wilderness that we did not, but we were willing to learn from anybody, and we had found that often the most unlikely people gave us information that was invaluable. I had learned a lot from old Pineys, and I had learned even more about deer from an old man who lived in the woods and fed hundreds of them every day. He could name more than a hundred deer by sight, and they would come up and eat out of his hand, although they would not even come close to me.

Rick and I walked back through the woods watching the clouds come in, dark gray with a brownish gray above, trailing long wisps of snow. Before we were fifteen minutes on the trail back, everything was covered with snow. We stopped on a rise about halfway along and looked back over the trail we had come up. The clouds hovered over the little valley behind us like a low roof, and the snow fell out of the clouds in one dense and continual stream so that there seemed to be a direct connection between the forest and the sky.

The curtain that hung there would eventually move, and when it did, going back toward the camp would be futile. Obviously, we would have to curl up when it overtook us. We could not travel too hard because if we began to sweat heavily, we would not be able to lie down and let the snow cover us up if the going got bad. Still we had no sense of being in danger. If worse came to worst, we could wait a little and dig into a snowbank. We were safe enough wherever we were. We could, if we gave it a little time, break enough pine branches in a few minutes to make a brush lean-to. Pine needles would keep a small fire going for the duration of the storm if we wanted luxury.

The storm caught up with us before we got back to camp. A white veil of fine, small grains kept falling and transforming everything. We wandered around mesmerized, watching it fall. We moved so erratically that it would have been hard to say when we were simply making side trips after something unusual and when we were lost. We spent too much time backtracking ourselves, and we did not get back until late in the day. But we were having a good time, and although the walking had gotten noticeably harder, we were moving through the woods like chickadees flying for the sheer joy of it.

Watching the storm from the luxury of lean-tos with bunks opening into the wind was going to be a treat, and to some extent, we looked forward to watching the storm in that kind of comfort, even if it did insulate us a bit from the true nature of the storm. You have to be *in* the storm to understand the sense of awe that fills the chickadee with joy. If watching from inside seemed like it was costing us the full experience of the storm, we could always go outside again.

We wondered if we would be able to talk somebody out of giving up the front bunks at the open face of the lean-to. Because we were new and they did not know our abilities, or because we were the youngest, they had put us in bunks at the low end of the sloping lean-to, closed off from the weather on all three sides. Rick didn't think we could get anybody to voluntarily give up a bunk with a great view for one that was all closed in like ours, but we reminded each other that we could always go outside if we wanted. What happened when we got back was incomprehensible to us.

The scoutmaster came toward us moaning and wringing his hands. "Oh, God, you're back," he said. "We thought you were already dead." I looked at Rick to see if he understood what the man was moaning about between his chattering teeth. But Rick couldn't understand him either.

"Who's dead?" we said. I noticed for the first time that the man's lips were blue and his face was wind-bitten. He looked as if he had been left laying on his face in the snow for an hour. His hands came out from under his armpits for the first time since we saw him and went waving around in the air like lunatics. "*We're* dead!" he shouted.

If he had not been an adult, I would have thought he was on the ragged edge of panic, but we had been having so much fun that it took me a minute to realize he was serious. "I can't get a fire going!" he moaned. "The wind's blowing! It's a blizzard." He sounded as if woe after woe had been piled upon him until he had begun to break. "We can't get the cars out!" He looked at us as if he were on the witness stand. "We only waited an *hour* and we couldn't get them out. We're going to die here if we don't get some help!" He shouted at us as if we were too stupid to grasp the enormity of our situation.

Then he began to look at us as if there was something odd about us he could not quite put his finger on. He went around us like a mother bird whose eggs have been disturbed. It was obvious that we weren't particularly cold, and we'd been gone a long time in the storm and didn't look any the worse for wear. The fact that we were warm, calm, and reasonable was probably what made him listen to us. That, and the fact that he was desperate.

"Well, do you want us to walk into town?" we said, and his hands went waving around again. "No! No! It's twelve miles or more!" Actually, it was only seven in a straight line, and we had walked further than that coming home from the Good Medicine Cabin sometimes. If we had known the true distance, we might have walked it. Instead we offered to do it when the storm settled. "We can't wait until the storm's over!" he said. "We need help now!"

He said it with the frenzy of a man who has forgotten to inform anybody about exactly where in the huge preserve he is going to be camped and who doesn't expect help for days at best. We looked into the lean-tos. They were open-faced garage-type affairs with a roof that sloped down toward the back. Each had ten Army spring cots in metal frames. All three were filled with boys huddling in their sleeping bags, crying or shivering or curled up quietly waiting to die. I could not believe it.

They had gotten the official word that they were going to die, and they had begun to prepare themselves in whatever way they could, but they had done nothing to survive. Even if they had all gotten together and huddled in a pile in the corner of one of the lean-tos, they would have had a much better chance of surviving. If they had given the extra sleeping bags to the outer layer of the pile, they could have kept warm that way.

We told the scoutmaster that we had been out in the woods in snow a lot of times before and that we could make a fire if he and the assistant scoutmaster could close off the front of the middle lean-to. Once he saw a direction, the scoutmaster calmed down and got all the scouts into the middle lean-to and laid picnic tables up against the front of the lean-to, leaving a space for us to make a fire.

By canting the tables out, we could use them as a reflector that would throw the heat back into the lean-to. Rick and I started our fire as we always did, with cedar shavings and with ground up pine needles. We chose for who would be the one to make the windscreen and I lost. Making the windscreen entailed opening your jacket like a pair of wings and settling down over the tinder like a bird roosting.

If you did not back up quick enough once the tinder caught, you got a hot stomach; and if you jumped back too soon, the fire went out. It was a delicate art and I got off a little late. But after I had slapped out the smoldering of my sweater we had the fire going, and before too long the lean-to was almost warm enough for everybody's taste.

After that, things got a lot easier as people warmed up and became useful again. We opened the tables out into reflectors and covered them with tin foil. As people got warm, we sent them out to gather wood. When it started to get dark, and most of the wood within easy reach had been gathered and burned, Rick and I took on the task of staying up all night and keeping the fire going.

We went off into the snow a little further each time, following our own markings and bringing back the wood. Whenever the sweat we worked up getting the wood started to become a gate to the cold, we would get back to the fire and cook up again before we went out to get some more. We watched the rolling whiteness build up until it looked like the woods were being flooded with white, slow-motion water.

All the time we gathered the wood, we looked up and watched the snow coming down and down and down, erasing the distant, dimming the close-at-hand. We watched the woods fill and fill, and we laughed at the sleepers with their heads hidden in their sleeping bags, missing everything the storm was bringing us. The winds had picked up even as we were walking back, and before light, the snow had stopped falling. But the wind was blowing so strongly that it didn't matter, and the woods filled faster and faster as the drifts collected passing flakes and set them to work catching others.

As it got lighter, we could see the tail of the storm going over us, and the winds scurrying along with it, stirring up the snow and reshaping it like an impatient artist working toward perfection. I watched the patterns form and unform as morning came up hidden somewhere behind the clouds. The snow was blowing a steady hiss of dying flakes into the fire. We stoked it more and more as the wind began blowing the heat off the flame tips.

We got sweaty working so close to the fire and our trips afield had to be made shorter and shorter. The storm was gone, but it had left behind a picture of the motion of the woods as it had passed, with every curve of that motion outlined in the tops of the snowbanks. The woods were quiet, except for the chickadees who seemed to be cheering in another storm or announcing that if they had survived another storm *without* cover, everyone under cover must surely have survived. They were in a sense the robins of winter announcing that rebirth is right around the corner.

Rick and I looked forward to a full day of tracking as the animals came out of cover to feed themselves. The sun came out about two hours later, and just as it did a huge Army truck came around the bend and down into the clearing. A guy in fatigues jumped out of the passenger's side and started waving his wool hat. ''Are you people all right?'' he yelled.

"Yeah," we yelled back, "We're having a great time." The guy let his hand drop and cocked his head and asked us what we had said. "We're fine," we yelled. "We'll be back on Tuesday!" The man shrugged and started getting back into the cab when the scoutmaster woke up and bolted out of the lean-to shouting, "Don't listen to them! They're crazy! Get us the hell out of here!"

So we did not get to track that part of the Pine Barrens until months later, but we got to go home and learn about the search that had been carried out for us. The scoutmaster gave us a lot of credit, and we were minor heroes for a short time. But it was all so simple that Rick and I took more than ordinary twelve-year-old pride in it.

We stayed in the Boy Scouts for a while because we became resident experts on nature, but we found that after a while we weren't learning anything new. There were no more winter campouts after that one, and we abandoned the Boy Scouts to spend our full time at our own exploration of the world. But it did not cease to amaze and worry me that those scouts would have died there through their own inaction if we had not told them the obvious. I resolved that when I eventually became a scoutmaster, my troop would be able to survive a blizzard with ease.

What we had done had been easy for us, but it still told us how far we had come in relation to people who had not been trained, and it made us realize that we had finished our apprenticeship and were ready to expand and use our skills. The fact that they had helped somebody made us feel good, and we looked thereafter for people we could help.

The woods seemed full of people after that, and we were always finding people who had gone too far off a major trail or who had wandered in circles for hours or days. Later that summer we passed a police car and a blue Ford on the shoulder of the road on our way out of the woods. We were practicing our stalking and we moved with the short burst of motion and slow catlike movements of the close stalk.

I came up silently behind the policeman and tapped him on the shoulder. He had his gun half drawn as he turned. After a few minutes of cursing and a ten-minute lecture on sneaking up on people like that, we found that the people in the car had stopped for a roadside picnic and their five-year-old had wandered away.

I had seen his tracks a little way up the trail and ordinarily, I would have followed them, but Rick and I were on our way home and we were already late. The rescue squad people had pulled up in their white bread truck and started milling around trying to get information, like ants bumping into one another. We said we could find him, and we showed them where his trail went.

They started crashing into the brush around the trail and covering the prints. Rick and I made our first discovery: it's easier to find somebody by yourself than with a lot of people who don't know what they're doing, getting in the way. The longer I track lost people, the clearer that becomes. If I get in before the five hundred searchers, the track is infinitely easier to follow and quite often the longest part of the search is finding the first footprint out beyond where the searchers have gone.

We got out in front of them as soon as we could and followed the trail. We moved a lot faster than they did, and we came on the boy sitting by a stream about a mile away. It felt good to have helped somebody, and we liked being the center of attraction and having the rescue squad give us coffee out of the truck, but the trail was of no great interest to us in itself. A human being in the woods usually isn't as interesting as a animal. Most people churn up the landscape only slightly less than a bear.

Later I would come to far more ambiguous human trails and far more interesting ones. But until I had done a lot more tracking, the trail of a person in the woods was of no further interest to me once I had established his business there, but the trail of an animal could lead to days of information and observation.

I was always amazed at the glint of absolute terror at

being lost that I found in the eyes of so many of the lost people. Once when I was hiking toward a camp in Lacey tract, I kept coming across the same car tracks, going down the same piece of road, sometimes two or three times a couple of days apart. I was never extremely interested in car tracks, except that they told me about the flow of outsiders in the pines, but I kept wondering if there was something wrong because the tracks went over each other so many times.

It was summer, and a lot of people came in off the roads who would not normally have gone into the woods. I thought it might be someone who had come into a place once and then tried to find it again a couple days later—but couldn't. But there was something that didn't seem right about the trail, but I could not quite put my finger on it. I found out what was wrong when I came out of the woods near a bend and saw a man cooking a little piece of meat on a charcoal grill.

There were a bunch of kids in the car crying and fighting, and his wife was crying even louder. I came up to him and asked if I could help him. He looked at me as if he was not sure I was real and then started stammering out questions too fast to keep up with. I told him that yes, I did know how to get out, and yes I would show him the way. He ran around to his wife's window and told her what she had probably overheard anyway. The crying quieted down and the man came back over and told me that they were vacationers from North Jersey who had come to the shore for a week and had decided to go on a picnic on their way home. They had thought it would be fun to spend their last day in the pines.

He said that they had gotten off the main trail and got turned around in the endless tangle of roads that all look alike until you've been down them a few dozen times. They had spent almost a whole tank of gas trying to find their way out. He had been parked where he was since the day before, when the gas tank had gotten too low to go any further without making it impossible to get out.

They had been sitting there in their own fresh tracks,

waiting unknowingly for their own car to come back down that road and save them. I didn't have the heart to tell them that they had probably been following their own freshly made tracks in circles the whole time.

I could see their trail in my mind, charging in a straight line for a while, then going in circles off it for a longer time, then going in a straight line again that curved into more circles. They could well have run out of gas and died wandering around on foot trying to get out. They had begun rationing their food the second day, and he had been cooking up the last of the meat. They were afraid to drink the water except when they were desperate. They did a lot of the right things, and they were lucky. Two or three people a year were not.

I told the man how to get out. He was only a twisting mile and a half from the main road, but he literally begged me to take him there instead of directing him because he was afraid he would get off the trail and never get back again. Naturally, I got in the car and drove out to the main road with them and saw them on their way. All the way out, they looked at the trees with abject terror. It was a concept I could not identify with.

There were many times, especially in the beginning, when I did not know where I was in relation to where I had started out, but I was never lost. At least I was not lost in the sense that I was someplace that I would not come back from unharmed. By the time we were going deep into the woods, Stalking Wolf had trained me so well that "lost" no longer meant anything. I could exist whenever I was in the Pine Barrens for as long as I needed to. I knew where food was, I knew where I could drink, and I had an infinite variety of things to watch. Everything I could want was immediately at hand. If I was lost, I seemed better off than a lot of people who weren't. I was always at home, wherever I was. Only when I came out of the forest did I find out how easy it was to get lost.

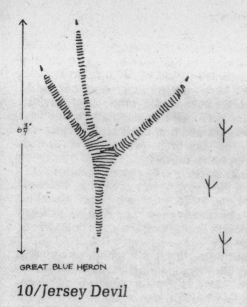

GREAT BLUE HERON

10/Jersey Devil

When Stalking Wolf gave us a test, it was not a test in the sense that it could be graded. It was a way of knowing what to work on next. The importance of the test was not the results but what we did with them.

This was always the case for Rick and me. All we cared about was the information, and a difficult failure often taught us more than two or three easy successes.

There were always two parts to the test, it seemed. One part tested some skill. Stalking Wolf made us run to keep up with him, and for a man as old as he was, he could move unbelievably fast. But there was another dimension to what he did. Stalking Wolf did not *say* we had to keep up with him, but if we didn't, we couldn't hear what he was saying. He improved our endurance while testing the limits of our commitment to knowing.

A limitless commitment to learning was less important than knowing the limits we had and what they were. Our training was a matter of defining our limits to ourselves as well as a way of sharpening our skills. Stalking Wolf taught us the basic principles of survival. The essential question anyone needs to ask to survive is "What do I need most and how can I get it?" Built into that question is the idea of knowing how much each thing is needed and how much each thing is worth. We learned those limits by testing, by experimentation.

We learned the limits of how many things we could break with our Kung Fu techniques by breaking things until we couldn't break any more; and then we accepted that as our temporary limit. We learned the limits of our hunger by testing it.

Given adequate water, it takes a month to starve to death in a book, but there are practical limits as well as theoretical ones. There is a point after which hunger either takes up the whole of your mind or becomes insignificant. We fasted until we found that after the second day it gets easier and easier, until you come to a point where you know the only thing that could stop your fast would be the bodily decay that comes with death.

We learned two things from our tests, the limits of our power and the limits of our will. One was a measurement of our skill and the other was the measurement of our personality. If we were in the woods and without food, we knew how long that fact would make us uncomfortable and how long before it would affect what we could do. We always knew how long before we would have to think in survival terms and that thinking allowed us to function normally in what would have seemed like life-or-death situations to anyone else. Most people underestimate their abilities because they have never had a chance to test their limits.

A lot of people panic in the woods because they think they are facing impossible obstacles. Almost universally, those who have survived impossible circumstances did not panic and found that they could survive far beyond what they normally thought of as their limits. We knew what our limits were, and we knew that there was probably a reserve behind them that would only come out when the crisis was for real.

How many boards, how many bricks, how fast, how far, how high—we were always finding out what our limits were and how far forward they had moved since the last time we measured them. Stalking Wolf set up our major tests and the most important of those came when we were twelve. There was a section of the Pine Barrens which we called Hell because it was almost without water, one of the very few areas like that in the Pine Barrens because the sandy soil makes it a natural watershed. Hell seemed hotter than anywhere else and harder to live in or walk through than it should have been. Exploring that area always tired us out more than exploring other places, and it was not a place we would have voluntarily spent the night.

I was still afraid then, but my fears stemmed more from the unknown than from the true physical dangers of being in the woods alone. The Jersey Devil, the huge hairy monster who lived uncatchable in the swamps and came out periodically to rob graves and kill people who blundered onto him, frightened me more than anything else. I had collected stories about the Jersey Devil from all of the old Pineys and each had a way of telling his stories that was so individual that nothing they said could be a lie.

I did not question the existence of the Jersey Devil; so many people had told me that he existed so much more vividly than people had told me he *didn't* exist, that it was easy for my twelve-year-old mind to see who was telling the truth. I thought of him with horror and, although I could keep that terror out of my mind enough to camp with Rick and to go into the woods alone, I had not yet camped out alone, except overnight.

There is something about camping out alone for a night that is different from camping out alone for a week. There are advantages to a long stay as I knew from camping for weeks with Rick. Because you become so familiar to the animals, life in the woods goes back to its normal routine and you see things that anyone who comes and stays a day or so cannot see.

But there were dangers as well. The solitude and the pure aloneness of being so far from any human communication was something to think about. But what troubled me most was that I would run into the Jersey Devil out there in the dark.

Stalking Wolf said that if we took our knives and camped in Hell for a week alone, we would never be afraid of anything again. He gave us strict instructions about what area we had to stay in and what trails we could use. If we saw another human being during our stay, we were to come back immediately and begin again at another time. We were allowed an area outside Hell with a stream running through it to fish in and get water from, but we had to make our camp in Hell and explore mostly within its limits.

Nowhere did my territory overlap Rick's. We were given a set of trails to go in by, and a separate set by which to come back out. But both our trails started and ended at a large pine tree in a clearing, where we were to meet Stalking Wolf on the eighth day. Rick and I wished each other luck and took off our separate ways.

It was late June, just after we got out of school, and the camping was easy. The trek for water was new the first few days and full of interesting detours. Thereafter I had landmarks, a lizard here, a mouse there, an owl, some rabbits to keep track of as I went by every day, and the trip was a pleasure instead of drudgery. But the nights were difficult.

I became good at making fires because the alternative was to be alone in the dark with the Jersey Devil. I learned to sleep soundly without sleeping at all by waking up with the crack of every branch until I could pick out the sound of a squirrel from the sounds of a deer. By the third night, I could sleep through without waking to the crack of every twig and the snapback of every branch.

That night I heard the first crack of a branch that had to be made by something walking upright. I came awake, as I had trained myself to do, with my knife in my hand. Out across the fire, something was moving that was not a deer or anything else on four legs. I was dead certain that it was the Jersey Devil. But before I could see it, it stopped—there was no more sound the rest of the night. I nodded at the fire with one hand on my knife and one on my throwing stick.

In the morning, it seemed to have been only a dream, and I went back to the pleasures of surviving. I went down into the lower part of Hell where there was a field of wild wheat and found a quail run. I bent down and when the quail came scurrying along, I threw the stick up the path so he had nowhere to run and nowhere to hide. I doubt that he even saw the stick coming. There is a harder method, sitting beside the run and striking down at the quail as it goes by, but it takes a lot more practice and gets messy if you're not quick. There is a third way, setting a short bow, a foot and a half high, next to the run and shooting the quail as it goes by with a very pointed three-pronged stick. The stick thrown straight down the run was the most primitive method and the best, if the quail didn't duck or see me leaning down.

I had a particularly good throwing stick, one that I had made from a knobbed root. It had a good heft to it and a nice easy motion off the hand. I threw that stick continually. When we were sitting around waiting for some special part of the day, I threw my stick more often than I did our Kung Fu exercises. I rarely missed with it. I took the quail back to the camp and ate it. By Stalking Wolf's rules, although we were allowed to leave Hell to hunt, we had to go immediately back when we were finished hunting. I also took back an eel that I had caught at the stream and some cattail roots to last me the rest of the week so I wouldn't have to go down there again. I might as well have been a muskrat.

When it started to get dark, I lost myself in careful preparations for supper. I put together my fire like a diamond cutter, and I worked continually to keep its size exact. I cooked up the stew in the shell of the snapping turtle I had caught the first day. I savoured it and tested it until the eating of it could not be put off any longer. I ate the fish slowly and pretended I did not see night coming down all around me.

Stars came out, a small portion of moon came up, but I went on with my meal as if it were still afternoon. I stayed up a long time feeding the fire in small precise amounts and I let myself nod off as I sat there. The crack of a branch snapped my head up.

I had no idea how long I had dozed off for I had no idea that I had even *moved*, until I found myself on my feet. I crouched there with my knife in one hand and my throwing stick in the other, spot-looking the four directions for attackers. I could hear it coming through the brush toward me, snapping branches out of its way as if it hated everything it came in contact with. I was frozen with terror and then I started jumping around and waving my knife at it to ward it off. I saw it only as a huge dark shadow coming out of the trees with a ghostly white luminescence around it. I *knew* it was the Jersey Devil.

I shrieked at it to make it go away, but it stayed and came closer. Before long it was too close for me to run. Anything that huge would surely run me down on uneven ground and tear me limb from limb. Part of what I did then was fear, and part was craziness, and part was simple knowledge of the way things survive. Mostly, though, it was a reflex that said, "When you're trapped and there's no other way out—attack!" Like the rabbit who goes berserk between the paws of the fox and escapes because the fox has no response for a rabbit that bites back. I took attack as my last hope for survival.

But on the rational level, I was totally convinced that I was going to die, torn to shreds, dragged away and eaten. I believed that it was so. Whatever was lurking at the edge of my firelight was about to kill me, and I had no escape. The fire flew higher and I thought I saw the creature, huge and hairy, just beyond the fringes of the light, watching me as if it wondered how I would eventually taste.

A miraculous thing happened to me at that moment. My fear turned itself inside out and became maniacal rage. I was still there and I was still scared, but I was too mad for fear to have any effect. I went flying into the darkness with my knife and stick flailing, screaming as I went.

But the thing retreated in front of me and stayed out of reach of my knife. It never slowed so much that I would risk the throwing stick to bring it down. I did not want to kill it or even fight with it; I only wanted to drive it off. Since it looked like the only way to risk a thing like that was to kill it outright, I went at it with everything I had.

I believe I must have chased it two hundred yards, well into the woods, before I fell down, too exhausted to run or punch or stab another time. I stayed on my hands and knees, panting, with my head hanging. I did not care if whatever I was chasing turned and came back on me all teeth and appetite. I did not care. I had spent my rage. I had spent my fear. I did not even care if death came quickly. There was nothing left to be afraid of. Eventually I looked up and there was nothing there.

In the morning when I got up, I found my tracks leading out of camp at a frantic run and leading back with a calm measured step, but there were no other tracks anywhere along the trail. There were no broken branches or snapped twigs where I thought I had heard them, and there were none of the breaks in the brush that something that big would have had to make, even going on all fours. There was no evidence that anything had been there, and yet I knew that I had seen what I had seen. I had chased something through the night.

I went back to camp and thought about it all day. I had seen something but nothing had been there. If it had been Stalking Wolf there would have been tracks surely, some sign that he had come to check up on me to see if I was all right and had not gone beyond my limits.

But there was no sign that anyone had been there, and no marks except my own. I came to the conclusion that what I had seen had been my own fear which had given ground and then fled entirely when I confronted it. I have not been truly afraid since.

My fear was gone. Stalking Wolf had been right. The rest of the stay was easy. I slept the whole night through. Nothing moved in the night. Nothing moved in my dreams. I slept in the arms of my natural reflexes certain that they would never let me down unless I interfered with them. I slept naturally, without anxiety.

The next day I made a fishhook out of some bones and went down and caught a pickerel. The day after I made a spearing trident and speared a catfish. He hung in the water, waving in the invisible wind of the current until I thrust a foot or so beyond his shape as Stalking Wolf had taught me and pierced him. The long thin point impaled him while the two side hooks kept him from wriggling away. Cleaned and cooked, the fish were delicious with a side order of cattail root and some sassafras tea. I ate like a king and put on weight.

Days were lazy, filled with easy summer pleasures. Cloud watching, bird watching, fishing. I went down to the sand and tracked grasshoppers as Stalking Wolf had once had us do. Along the sandy places between bushes there were little scratches in the dust where they sat, where they leaped, and where they landed. The legs told me the direction, I knew roughly how far they could jump, and I simply laid out a straight line and moved my face along it until I came to the next set of tracks.

I caught a handful of them out of the bush and took them to a bare spot 20 or 30 yards in any direction from the nearest bush. I sat with my eyes closed for half an hour waiting for them to get where they were going. Then I followed the marks crawling carefully to avoid other prints until I found the bushes each of them had gone to. I chose the most popular bush, and caught a whole shirtfull out of it. I took them back to camp, cooked them, and ate them. I thanked the spirit-that-moves-in-all-things for showing me the excess that could be taken without damage. I stayed my days, being fed out of the pattern of the woods, until it was time to go.

When the eighth day came, I could have easily stayed another seven, or another seventy. I had come to like being alone so much that I did not ever want to go back. But on the eighth day, I took my knife and restored my camp as much as I could and went back toward the pine tree where Stalking Wolf was waiting for us.

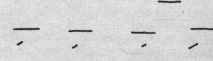

GRASSHOPPER IN DAMP SAND

INDIAN STYLE WALK
PLACING ONE FOOT IN FRONT OF THE OTHER

11/Invisible Walking

I got up just before sunrise, but I did not leave Hell until much later in the morning. We were to meet Stalking Wolf at noon, and I did not want to be early for fear of seeming like I wanted to get out of there. I knew that in his camp, Rick was probably doing the same. There was no need to rush, and there seemed to be even more things to see than usual.

I was not even certain that it was time to go back, and I had to sit for a while counting off the days by their events, Root Sunday, Gopher Day, the day of the grackle fight, three Jersey Devil days, and one to celebrate. I was in the morning of the eighth day, the day we were to meet Stalking Wolf at noon under the Clearing Pine.

Leaving was a mere formality. I could have stayed

there as long as I wanted or needed to. My fear was gone, and I had found that living there was easy compared to what I had expected. Once I was no longer on the verge of letting panic steal my wits, everything came easily. But even when the snap of a twig tore me out of my soundest sleep in heart-squeezing terror, I had been able to survive.

I had done the daily things that must be done to keep alive, even when all I could think about was the coming of night and the Jersey Devil sitting somewhere digging his claws into a fallen log and watching the sun set. I did what needed to be done. I had survived, and when I finally learned to let my instincts and my training do their work, things had gotten easy.

The last part of the week had been a festival. The more I looked at the emptiness of Hell, the fuller it got. When it was time to go, I promised myself I would come there again often because I was leaving behind so much that I had not had time to explore thoroughly enough. It was one of those times when what I did felt *so right*, that there was no need to ask Stalking Wolf for confirmation.

Even if he told me to come back again and look harder, even if the fact that I had had no vision made me take the test again, I knew that I had done exactly and completely what I had needed to do. I had the sense of relief that comes from knowing that you have done the hardest of all the things you have to do, and the independence that comes from having done something very difficult and important to yourself, even though no one else thinks it's the least significant. I had met my fear, foolish though it had been, and I had conquered it.

It did not matter if what I had seen was only Stalking Wolf come to check up on me. Through the distortion of my fear, what I saw was truly the Jersey Devil, and if the Jersey Devil of legend had come in the flesh toward me, I would have acted no differently. The fact that my triumph might seem trivial to anyone else did not diminish its magnitude for me.

I knew that things might still frighten me from time

to time, but nothing could set me flying into that blind panic out of which the prey is almost always taken. I was not vulnerable in that way any more, and it opened up important new worlds for me. New worlds I wanted to explore in their entirety, starting where I was. But I did not want Stalking Wolf to think that I did not have the skill to come back when I should. I restored as much of the landscape as possible and started down the trails, taking them in the exact order they had been given. I was going out a different set of trails than I had gone in, leaving behind the frightened little boy who had come into the woods a week before.

My fear would always exist in those woods, but it would have no power over me any more. I would be able to pass it within touching, without a frightened glance. The world had been greatly changed, and I did not make the time I should have, leaving as late as I did. Everything seemed so wondrously different from what it had been a week earlier that I kept stopping and looking around, trying to take it all in at once in some way that would make it indelible. I wanted to hold forever the woods as they were, impossibly new and bright.

And yet I was troubled because I had not had my vision. I had seen a number of beautiful and significant things, but nothing I had seen had so stunned me that I would know it for an omen. That omission disturbed me as I went down the trails, but it did not fog my attention to what was around me, nor did it make me any less grateful for what I had been lucky enough to experience.

I did not realize that there was no necessity for my vision to come to me in a dream, nor for it to come while I was in Hell. Possibly, I wandered as much as I did because I wanted to find that rare sight that is so perfectly balanced, so perfectly composed, that you know it cannot be the work of chance or some blind force stirring up life in a random pattern. I was coming through a cedar swamp when I saw it.

I had expected something exciting and dangerous,

and I was not prepared for what I saw. The light came in slantwise through the cedar skeletons in long flat blades. A short steep waterfall dropped like a shaft of ice and beside it on a bed of moss, invisible in a semicircle of bushes, was a small, tan fawn. The light came down on it like a spotlight and some of it hit the waterfall and burst into star-shaped rainbows. The beauty of it made the tears roll down my cheeks, and I felt greatly honored and yet greatly humbled. I watched it until a cloud came and shut off the light for a second, and when the rays shot back into the glade, the fawn was gone. I moved away as quietly as if it were still there.

The shaft of light still crackled with sunbeams and the mist from the waterfall flattened and hung along the water. It seemed to glitter still with perfect *rightness*, like a flawless motion in the newer perfected part of some pattern working its way toward complete perfection. I had seen the spirit-that-moves-in-all-things moving through the woods, and it touched me in a way that has shaped me ever since. Every day I work toward being part of the miracle whose glory has not faded over all these years. In everything I do I hope to see the motion of that force moving everywhere at once as I saw it once near that waterfall, for only an instant.

When I looked up to get the time, the sun was a white-yellow disc behind clouds that looked like puffy gray paving stones. Sunlight ran down between them like melted gold pouring through the cracks in the floor of the sky. I was a little behind where I should have been, and I moved up the trail picking up my wonders on the fly.

By the time the sun was right overhead, I was just coming into the clearing. Rick was coming into it from the far side, but we did not laugh or wave or come shouting toward each other as we would have a week before. We smiled and walked solemnly toward the Clearing Pine. But Stalking Wolf was not there.

I wanted to tell Rick everything that had happened to me, but I had the feeling that he already knew, that he had, in his own way, been touched by the same inexplicable beauty, and that he had triumphed over his own personal demons in the dark. The clearing seemed different somehow, as if it was a stage instead of a live place. Rick seemed to sense it too, because he did not laugh or wave even when we got close. We looked for Stalking Wolf, but he was not there, and we went toward the tree to see if he was not hiding on the side of the trunk away from both of us.

But when we got to it and went all around it, we did not even find his tracks. We were puzzled; it was not at all like Stalking Wolf to be late for something as important as that. It never occurred to us that he might be sick or hurt. His age alone seemed proof to us that he was indestructible. I wondered if perhaps Rick and I had both miscounted the days, and I had a picture of Stalking Wolf coming the next day and telling us that we had to start all over because we had seen another person before our time was up. But it was unlikely that we were both wrong about the day and we sat down under the tree to wait.

Much as I wanted to tell Rick everything that had happened, it did not seem right to speak out loud there at that moment. I could see Rick bubbling with the same mysteries, but we sat in silence for a long time. Finally, I saw the twig at the edge of the clearing. It was bent intentionally in the form that Stalking Wolf had told us meant, "Something important! Here!" I was up and running toward it two steps sooner than Rick, but he got there first anyway.

What we found was a perfect, newly-made footprint that we knew had to belong to Stalking Wolf. There were more prints backward down the trail, but they stopped at the edge of the clearing. We went all around the outside of the clearing looking for signs, but there was no print or mark anywhere around the perimeter.

We scoured the whole clearing and even the tufts of grass. The print was fresh; if he had walked on the ground, he had left no mark and if he had walked on the patches of grass, he had not bent it down. The footprint was too fresh for the grass to have come back up the way it was. We sat down again under the tree to puzzle it out. Stalking Wolf's voice broke from above us like thunder out of a clear sky.

My heart doubled up, but I did not startle. The voice seemed to come out of the sky. "A week ago, I saw two boys walk into the woods," the voice said; "today I saw two men come back out." Stalking Wolf came down the tree like a squirrel and stood in front of us. He said nothing, but his hand moved in eloquent patterns that told us that what had happened to us was our own personal vision, and I knew what the hand meant.

When he had finished, Stalking Wolf smiled and whatever ritual had passed between us was over. Rick and I jumped up together and started asking him how he could have gotten across the clearing without leaving tracks. He turned and walked softly back across the clearing with Rick and me a few feet behind him watching him go backwards from tuft of grass to tuft of grass, pulling the trampled grass up behind him with a twisting motion that made it spiral perfectly back into place.

He moved so lightly that only part of his weight seemed to be pushing against the ground at any one time, and where he could not reach a tuft of grass, his hand moved like a brush over the footprint and it was gone except for a faint rustle of dust that might as easily have been windblow. I believe I could have practiced all my life without being able to walk that way as well as Stalking Wolf. We followed him out of the clearing; he went a mile or more without leaving a trace. The fact that a man could go through the world without leaving a trail was a miracle to us, and we followed Stalking Wolf out of the clearing with awe.

On the way back to the Good Medicine Cabin, we practiced invisible walking on all kinds of terrain until Stalking Wolf was satisfied that we understood the principles. Rick had the light, swift movement of his grandfather, and he left a lighter trail than I did. He was faster at it because I could see so many more nuances to the track than he could, and I spent too much time covering up things that almost nobody else would be able to see. I was too meticulous to be as fast as Rick, but I got good speed at it after a while.

Thereafter, about half the time we went across any grassy place, we took up our tracks behind us, and if we had nothing better to do, we would go and clear our prints from the trails around where we were. Once when Stalking Wolf was supposed to come out with us for the weekend, we erased all our prints from the trail with the most meticulous care. We went over it again when we were finished, using all the little techniques we had invented erasing the other prints. We worked the whole week, and when he came out, he stopped about 50 feet from where our first print had been and smiled as if we had tried to play an obvious joke on him.

I believe he was pleased that we had done such a meticulous job, even if our erasures were like blotches where our prints should have been. Still, I wondered how he had known where we had started, and I asked him. "I looked," he said. I had the feeling that he was trying not to laugh.

"Yes, Grandfather," I said, "but what did you *see*?"

"Nothing," he said.

"Well, what was disturbed then?" I asked.

"Nothing," he said. I knew the answer was going to be obvious forever once I found it. "You look," he said when I started to ask another question, and we went up the trail. It looked perfect to me. Even I couldn't tell where our prints had been and I had spent a week erasing them. There was nothing that could have given us away. Nothing!

I was another hundred yards up the trail before I realized that *nothing* was exactly what had given us away. In our zealousness, we had erased *every* track from the trail—rabbit, fox, opossum, squirrel. We had created a highway of nothing in the middle of all that life. We might as well have painted the trail red to hide our prints.

When we got to the cabin that day, Stalking Wolf told us that he was going back to his reservation and would not be back until the end of summer. I had the feeling that he thought he might not be coming back at all, and I was worried when October came and he had not returned. But he was back in November, and the worry was for nothing.

I believe he sensed my fear and decided on the ceremony as a way to make me understand that our friendship was a special bond that could not be damaged by time or distance. It was not, I believe, a common ceremony, but when it was over I felt that in all important ways he was still with us, even when he left. I believe Stalking Wolf selected it to make a point that could not easily be put into words, and its effect on us was permanent and profound.

We sat near the campfire in front of the Good Medicine Cabin. Even the darkness seemed to shine when the moon came up. Stalking Wolf spoke in his own language, and his hand moved like years and firm foundations. Then we passed the knife and laid the blade against the pad of our palm and pressed it down with our fingers until it bit just deep enough. Stalking Wolf put his palm outward and Rick and I put ours against it. Then he bound our hands together with a strap of soft leather, and we sat for a long time smoking Stalking Wolf's own preparation of herbs and tobacco in a hand carved pipe made out of clay and bones.

His hand, after it passed the pipe, told us that our true selves lived in the blood, and that what was mingling was not simply our blood but our spirits. The process of the ceremony bound us together in unbreakable ways. Stalking Wolf undid the strap slowly, and as the last twist of it dangled in the air from his hand, a huge buck walked slowly into our camp.

We had not moved since the pipe had settled in Stalking Wolf's lap which might have been hours before. The buck came out of the cedar swamp like an advanced scout clearing an area. He came through our camp at a slow walk, checking from side to side, nosing in our gear, and yet he walked right past us as if we weren't there. At the far side of the clearing, he stopped and looked back. Out of the low mist of the swamp, the deer came bounding in long slow arcs, tumbling after one another like waves stacked behind each other by a storm. Four doe and two fawns came gliding like the moving parts of the same creature across the clearing. They seemed to flow into the air, landing softer than ballerinas and leaping again as if they intended to leave the planet.

When the last of them had bounded beyond the glow of our fire, the buck gathered himself like a storm cloud and sprang up and over the bushes into the dark. Stalking Wolf's hand rose like a benediction. "The spirit-that-moves-in-all-things," he said, "has shown us great favor. Invisibility is a great gift." And it was true. To have been invisible even for a moment was great good fortune. To be invisible outside of the miracle was hard work.

We worked constantly on being invisible. Stalking Wolf taught us its secret. Passing unobserved is indistinguishable in practical terms from being invisible. We learned the principles of passing unobserved. Be still. Be silent. Conform to the shape of what surrounds you. Take advantage of the shadows and places where the light makes things uncertain. Stand *above* whenever possible; most things do not look up, deer rarely do.

If you want to be invisible to humans in the woods, he taught us, keep your profile below chest level. Look around trees, rocks, and other obstacles close to the ground, not at eye level. We practiced every technique, but it was not until we learned to blend in mentally with the woods that we became as good as invisible.

We practiced constantly, working to make ourselves as good as invisible even when we moved. A flowing motion is harder to observe against the background of the woods than an erratic or eccentric one. One of the things that attracts predators to the sick and injured is the way the motion of their bodies clashes with the flow of the motion around them. "Move as the wind moves," Stalking Wolf had taught us, and we made our motion flow like the movement of leaves on wind-bent branches. Even around the house we practiced, getting up and fitting our walk in behind someone who went past. Walking in their footprints as their feet moved out of them, our legs almost touching theirs, we would glide invisibly behind our parents and our friends dropping off before they turned to see us and slipping into a shadow or into a chair as if we had been sitting in it all the time. We drove everyone crazy, including each other, popping out of nowhere, rising out of the shadow of a tree or a wall, appearing suddenly in the middle of a conversation to the surprise of whoever was standing there.

When I moved right, when the precision of my training blended perfectly with the pattern around me, I could catch out of the corner of my eye a faint halo of the glory that had come to me with my vision. I could see it shining out of all things like the bright shadow of the spirit that moved beyond them.

WOODCHUCK   FORE   HIND

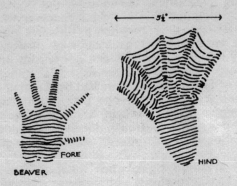

BEAVER — FORE — HIND

12/True Lostness

Rick and I were inseparable. When anyone saw one of us, they were sure the other was around somewhere, and nine times out of ten they would be right. Even when one of us went somewhere alone, the other got a report of it as soon as we got together again. We shared everything.

At the time, the only human being in the world who knew what was really going on in my life and understood it was Rick. There was too much I could not share with my parents for fear of frightening them into keeping me out of the woods, and only a true nature fanatic like Rick would have understood the importance of much that I might have told them.

A good portion of most children's lives are invisible to their parents. It's inevitable. Kids have to take risks to grow up, and parents have a natural instinct to limit the risks their child can take. So, most boys take to living private lives in which they risk going beyond their limits to find out what their limits are. Rick and I lived the bulk of our time together. It made for a closeness that is almost never found in adulthood.

We had only one falling out in the whole time I knew him, and it was, I believe, an example of what I think of as "true lostness." True lostness had nothing to do with the woods or the wilderness; in fact, the times I have been most truly lost in my life, I was almost always living outside the woods. True lostness is when you have forgotten the spiritual center of your life, when your values have gotten so warped with time that you do not remember what is truly important. With Rick and me it happened with skulls.

In the beginning, the skulls were treasures brought back to remind us of great adventures or the vastness of what the woods had to teach us. The center of our lives was the understanding of nature. Skulls were a part of our study. We collected them, identified them, analyzed them. They were a part of the woods that we could carry around with us, into school, at home, anywhere we needed. When city life and permanent rules crowded in on us, we needed a piece of nature to sustain us. Skulls were good medicine, something sacred because of its correspondence with something greater. The skulls were a direct link with nature that kept us in contact with the true center of our lives.

The process by which we lost that link was gradual, and I doubt that even an introspective adult would have noticed it. It occurred because we focused so intently on the skulls that they took on an importance in themselves and not for what they could teach us about nature. Gradually, we stopped collecting specimens of nature and started collecting *skulls*!

It was not long after that that we began to spend more time at home with our collections than out in the woods collecting. When we went out in the woods, we could not get out of the back of our minds that we might find a skull. When one of us did find one, the other was happy for him but envious. Inevitably we came to the perfect skull, and both of us reached for it at once.

We argued of course, the greed for skulls making us blind to anything else. I let him pick it up having no idea he would try to claim it; he picked it up thinking I was acknowledging his right to keep it. We fought over it all the way home, and when Rick took it into his house with him after an especially bitter exchange, we were no longer speaking to one another.

For a while, our collections sustained us. We went every day to school on the same bus but we never talked, except to taunt one another with the number of skulls in our collections or the rarity of a skull we had just found. When we passed each other in the woods, we did not even nod. And we passed each other continually, because we were constantly in the woods. It was as if each of us was afraid the other was going to beat him to all the good skulls. We missed most of what was around us because of our greed for skulls. We stopped looking up or around, skulls were found on the ground, we looked nearer and nearer to our feet. Gradually, we passed each other without even looking up. We passed everything else the same way. The trails might just as well have wound through factories for all we looked around us. It took something spectacular to shake me out of that stupidity.

I was going down into a marsh where I had not been before and I found the only beaver mound I had ever seen. Rick and I had always wanted to observe beaver, but we had never found any. It was an incredible opportunity, and I bent down to look inside. There were no beaver alive to watch, but I found the next best thing, three full skeletons. I shouted for pure joy and turned to tell Rick. He wasn't there of course. I felt like the last person on earth.

Rick was the only one who could really understand what fantastic luck it was to find not one but *three* full skeletons. Usually all we found was a bone or a piece of bone. We treated even the smallest bone with reverence.

When we found a bone we would rope off the area with strings and twigs. Then, we'd sit off from it a little and observe it undisturbed, making estimations about what part of what animal it was. Then we'd try to figure out what happened to it. The tracks were usually long gone by then, but sometimes there was a bit of fur or a feather that could give us a clue to guess from.

Usually the body had been attacked by dogs, and we'd have to follow the tracks all over the place looking for the next bone, which might be 100 yards away at the next spot the dog lay down to rest. That was why the skulls were so precious. Skulls were almost always carried away to be eaten, the brain left for last and carried home like ice cream. To find a whole skeleton in one piece was worth a kingdom. Three were worth an empire.

There was nothing to do but go and find Rick. I did not really care what I would have to say to him to be his friend again. The skull was nothing. He could keep it. We had wasted too much time over it as it was. As I ran looking for Rick, the woods was visible to me for the first time in weeks. Everywhere I looked things seemed to have leaped ahead in time. Important changes in the greenery had come and gone unnoticed. I felt as bad about having lost that as I did about having not shared it with Rick. But I cheered myself with the thought that we would not lose any more wonders out of pigheadedness and greed. Rick could have all my skulls if he wanted, as long as we got back to watching nature.

I knew Rick was down in a swamp about a mile and a half away because I had seen him on the way in. I had gone by him grumbling to myself that he would get the good skulls first. It seemed ridiculous to me as I ran, that I had been that foolish. I took the widest trail to make the running easier. There were shorter routes but the wide trail would be fastest. Running did not diminish my excitement. Three whole skeletons! And *beaver* at that! Rick went running by me in the opposite direction.

I was two steps past him before it hit me and I almost

tripped trying to turn and call after him against my momentum. He did the same thing, and we stumbled toward each other, too out of breath to speak and almost too exhausted to point and grimace. Rick kept panting and making funny faces and pointing to the swamp. His face was so contorted trying to catch his breath and talk at the same time that the only thing I could think of was that he was trying to tell me that he'd seen the Jersey Devil in the swamp.

I got my breath first, but the Jersey Devil took precedence over even beavers and I gasped, "Did you see him in the swamp?" Rick looked like he thought he must have missed something, and I said, "The Jersey Devil!"

Rick's eyes got wide. "You *saw* him."

"No!" I said, "You did." Rick looked at me as if I was crazy, but he was starting to laugh.

"What?!!" he said.

I had gotten my breath back, but I was starting to laugh too and I was having as much trouble talking as before. "You were making faces and pointing in the swamp," I said. "I thought you were trying to tell me you saw the Jersey Devil." Rick fell over laughing, and I let myself collapse as well; I knew everything was going to be all right.

I don't know how long we laughed, but it was one of those things where whenever one of us would stop, he would hear the other and start up again. We were like two flocks of birds starting each other up with their warning cries.

I had seen that happen once for twenty minutes. A fox startled one flock, and they started sending our cries and alarms and woke up the second flock, who took up the cry. When the first flock quieted down, it heard the second flock giving warning cries and they started up again to pass the warning along. When the second group stopped they heard the first, and so on. I don't know how they finally figured out there was nothing out to be screeching and scolding about.

Rick stopped as abruptly as the birds had. "The robins!'' he said and jumped up. He pulled me to my feet. "Hatching robins!" he said and we started off down the trail at a dead run. Rick was always a faster runner than I was, but he ran a little below top speed for me to keep up. He could have just told me where they were and then sprinted on ahead not to miss them. But he waited for me to see it too, and that was something only a friend would do.

When the eggs were hatched, we got to talking about how rotten it had been without anyone to share the important things with. Eventually, the only thing left to say was, "Let's just forget that, and thank God we're friends again." And then I remembered the beaver skeletons. Rick seemed to think about them at the same time, and he asked me where I was running to when I passed him. I said I had been looking for him to show him something fantastic. But I wouldn't tell him what it was. I said I'd show him instead.

Rick was astounded when he looked into the beaver mound. "Two!"

I shook my head. "*Three*!" I said, "You can have the other one if you want." Rick shook his head, and we came to the agreement that everything we collected was to be held in common ownership. Anything one of us found belonged to the other as well.

We shook hands on it. It was, I believe, an awkwardness left over from the split, but it was the last effect the argument had on us, other than to teach us how easy it was to become as greedy and grasping as everyone else seemed to be. We recognized ruefully how little we had valued the important things, like our friendship and everything that was going on in the woods. Rick had also been struck, as he ran, by the changes that had gone on unnoticed all around him. I believe that was what put the skulls back into perspective for us, and we turned to the beaver mound, not as collectors, but as observers of nature.

What we saw was a nightmare. Further in the den there were six other skeletons, all perfectly preserved, all dead, we thought at first, by poison, but there was no smell of it. As we hauled the skeletons out we came to see them less as skeletons, beautiful though they were to us, and more as animals, other vulnerable creatures wiped out by some disaster.

When we explored the area we understood how they had died. There had been an aspen grove not far away. In its place there was a cement drainage embankment. Beaver love aspen. They can eat other things, but they ignore everything else if they can find aspen. These beaver had intended to use the aspen grove as their reserve food supply. When their inside stores were almost used up, they went out to find that the whole grove was under some construction company's bulldozer. They must have gone back with their tails down and ate what they had left. The ice must have caught them before they got out again, and they were too weak from hunger then to break through it. Or perhaps they just went home and lay down and died with as much dignity as they could. It was a small family tragedy.

But it was like the end of the world to us. By the time we had taken all of the skeletons out, we were shaking with rage. There were nine of them in all, dead in their skins. Nothing but bones. They must have been a long time in there dying. We ran at the sewer pipes and threw rocks at them and screamed at them and cursed their owners, but they were huge cement things that paid us no attention. It was the first time I had felt truly helpless before the web of greed that passes for human society. If I could have blown up the sewer pipe, and the company that made it, and the politician who approved of it, and the company that put it in, and the company it had been put in for, I would have.

Instead, we took the last bit of money we had and bought a can of black spray paint and went up and down that sewer pipe, indicting them for nine murders, cursing their ancestry, and damning them to a premature bankruptcy. All along the pipes we went, demanding vengeance for the dead, until the paint was gone and we had run out of words.

There were no words big enough for our sorrow or our rage, and we took the can and disposed of it when we got back, where cans belonged. It didn't matter much anyway, and we knew that. If they ever saw the words, they wouldn't have understood them and if they had understood them, they wouldn't have cared. And if they cared, they would have just told us that they were just doing their jobs.

The same people who brought the sewer pipes turn another small piece of the Pine Barrens into money every few weeks. Probably when there's nothing left, and the last of the watershed is poisoned, the people who are responsible for killing the beaver will know the helpless sense of irreversible loss Rick and I had felt. But that's a long time from now, years at least.

I doubt that anyone saw the paint anyway. The pipes were below the level of the highway and couldn't be seen from the road. I doubt anyone went down to look at them. They wouldn't have paid attention to what we wrote anyway. It was all misspelled.

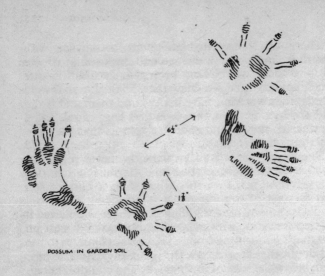

POSSUM IN GARDEN SOIL

13/Predator

There was no greater test of our invisibility than the deer. Sometimes when we stalked animals, they heard us coming or caught our scent, but I don't believe any animal saw us coming, except the deer. Deer were always difficult. Their eyesight was good and their sense of smell even better, but their hearing was better than both, and they had an uncanny sense of what was going on around them in the woods. They were the true test of the predator.

They were my test as well, and I went in to hunt my deer with only a knife. I had stalked him for a week, letting the woods so match the course of our actions that our final meeting would be inevitable. I moved in the dark part of the pattern, waiting for the woods to bring us together, waiting for the inevitable to ripen. I sat in the summer pine lashing my knife to a short stick with bullbriars. Rick and I had pulled the thorns off the briars to make twine. They were stronger than leather when used right. I lashed the knife to the stick and tested its firmness.

The branch dipped and rose faintly as I moved, and a jay in a nearby tree started its alarms, raising a commotion until any creature who was interested could locate me and stay away. I heard its racket with the annoyance every predator does. If it stayed there all day without getting used to me, I might have to climb down and find another tree further up the run.

I did not really want to be in the tree, but I believed it was necessary and I believed it was correct. We were on a long survival campout. We had a whole summer to use the meat, and what we didn't use could be used at home. There was every reason for killing the deer, and I had no qualms about killing for food. It was part of the pattern everywhere I looked.

Still, I had reservations about what I would have to do. I was a day hungry, but I was not really starving. I could always walk far enough to beg food if eating was all that there was to it. But I knew there was more to it than that. The woods had something else to teach me, and my hunt had another purpose that I was not aware of. If my hunt was wrong, the forest would send me no deer to be killed. I waited patiently all day long, paying attention to how the ground changed as the day progressed and watching the weather as I could see it through the branches. There was a comfortable branch to rest my chin on, and the jay got used to me or went off duty. Sunset came and I caught a small patch of it over my shoulder, out through the pines.

Then it was dusk and I could hear my deer coming softly, looking around as if he knew I was there somewhere. Maybe he was seeing that tree standing out like an omen and was shying back from it. But eventually he came under the tree, and whatever pattern we were stuck in wound itself tighter. The force that moved in both of us moved the deer under me and I dropped.

The buck staggered when I landed on his back and would have bolted, but I pulled its head back by the antlers and stabbed down into its chest. I stabbed him again and he started to drop. The dying took forever, and he would not go fully down. I pulled out the knife and jerked his head back and slit his throat. But he still wouldn't go down and I realized that it was no ordinary deer.

He kicked and bucked and wrenched his head around, jabbing at me with his antlers. I started to slide off his back and he pranced around my dangling feet as if he was trying to step on them. He kicked me twice before I tripped him to the ground and stabbed him all the way through. All the way in, I could feel the terrible force of predation driving my hand and I understood how it was to be part of the dance of eater and eaten that made up so much of the flow of the woods. I thanked the spirit of the woods for sending me such a strong and noble adversary to teach me my lesson.

The deer was a promise that if I was ever desperate, nature would provide me with what I needed as everything else was provided with food and a purpose. I cherished it. Rick and I skinned it and I made a robe from the skin as Stalking Wolf's ancestors would have done. The meat we ate or salted, and we took some of it home. The feet we kept for making tracks, and the antlers I made a knife of except for one branch that I made into a medicine necklace.

We cured the hide in Pine Barrens water, and I made a ladle out of the skull, cleaning and packing it with clay before I set it in the fire to harden. When it was done, I rubbed it with pitch and set it near the fire until the pitch bubbled. Then I took it away and let it cool until it was ready to use. Every part of the deer was used, and everything we made from it was permeated by our reverence for the sacrifice the deer had made for us.

I have killed no deer since then except for food and then only after all other alternatives have failed. I hunt with a camera now because I believe that the forest had a twofold purpose in bringing my deer and me together.

Human beings are predators, and that is a fact that can only be understood in the way I came to understand it. But the agonies of the kill stayed with me, and I believed that the forest had made me a present of death so that I would avoid inflicting it in the future.

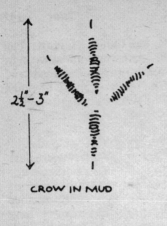

2½"–3"

CROW IN MUD

4½"

14/Thaw

We had been men for a long time when we set out at dusk for a night stay on the slope of Forked River Mountain. We were afraid of nothing, but being on hard-topped road made us edgy. There was no other reason for the conversation except perhaps the fact that it was one of those days when everything seemed eerie. The swamp had a fog coming off it that whisped across the macadam road and made it seem even more forbidding.

At sunset, there seemed to be crows everywhere we looked. They were sleek, beautiful birds, but when they cawed, their voices had a strange horror movie echo to them. The ground had frozen, then thawed under some unusually warm weather for January, and had then refrozen, forming cracks and bubbles in all the tracks

146

and making them look as if they were diseased. The ground was hard again and newer prints were light shadows over solid impressions formed during the thaw, and it made the present look like the ghost of some unrelenting past. The ground was a good 10 degrees from unfreezing, but it seemed on the verge of it anyway.

The sunset was pink with a lot of low gray clouds that came in and choked it off; the crows that flew were dark shadows against dark gray. We saw four opossums and a squirrel dead along the road, but instead of angering us, the remains depressed us. So many things seemed slightly off key. It was the kind of feeling I have whenever something is not right in the woods. Birds seemed to have turned in early or become mute. When I saw the swamp, instead of thinking of the time I saw a Brown Marsh Hawk come gliding in over the tops of the cattails there, I thought of the mist coming off horror-film graveyards. That was not the kind of association I would normally make, and I thought that I was just in some quirky mood that would pass when we were deeper into the woods.

But if it was a mood, Rick seemed to have caught it too. The fog must have made him think of the same thing, because he said, "You remember the foot we found in that graveyard that time?" I knew which graveyard he meant, the old black graveyard behind a decayed building that was a church before it became a wildlife sanctuary.

We had explored the ruin and then had gone into the graveyard behind it. The bodies were buried without caskets, paupers' graves most of them, and a really hard rain would sometimes turn up a corpse for the dogs. There were two bodies up when we went in. The dogs had gotten to one and the first indication that they were there was when Rick leaned over to read a tombstone and found the foot. One of the dogs had dragged it there to avoid sharing it no doubt. We left it where it was and moved through the graveyard toward a phone where we called the police.

It hadn't really bothered us. We had been investigating dead things since the beginning. There had been a whisp of fog in the cemetery that night too. If it did bother us, neither would have shown it anyway. All of our training said we were to express no fear. An Indian is not afraid. A Kung Fuist is not afraid. We were not afraid. The foot had been trivial.

"What about it?" I said.

"Nothing," he said.

Then he didn't say anything for a while. We were getting further into the woods and that was making me feel better, but we were losing the light in a very intermittent way because of the clouds, and the quiet seemed excessive for a night that still hadn't hit much below freezing all day.

We walked for a long time before Rick said anything else. "You remember the cedar swamp?" he said. I smiled. When we were littler, we used to sit and tell each other ghost stories until we had thoroughly scared ourselves. It's always in the imagination that fear makes its easiest bed, and by the time we were ready to go into the cedar swamp, we were convinced that it was the one cedar swamp in all New Jersey where the Jersey Devil lay waiting to rip to shreds the first living thing that walked into his territory. No matter who went in, the other would stalk up on him and give the most bloodcurdling bellowing scream he could. We never went in very far to begin with, and we came back out a lot faster than we went in.

"Yeah," I said. "What was the record for staying in there, you remember?" Rick shrugged and said fifteen minutes. I said it was more like five. Rick nodded and said that the record was probably fifty seconds and it had only seemed like five hours. We both laughed and things seemed to lift a bit. The heavy quality went out of the air, and the stars went back to being crisp January stars.

We started walking faster, and I saw a bat do its broken-winged dance across the rising moon. The twitter of its flight was always a joy to watch, and it kept me smiling until we got to the foot of Forked River Mountain. Forked River Mountain isn't even really a hill, but southern New Jersey is a flat, low place, and a hundred feet of elevation can let you see across a rolling sea of pines as far as Atlantic City and beyond.

We never missed a chance to look at it, and we went up the mountain before making camp. The clouds had blown over, and we could see the lights of Atlantic City down the shaded dark to the southeast. The trees had a faint glow to them as they always seemed to. Scientists called it Pine Barrens phosphoresence. We thought of it as the breath of the spirit-that-moves-in-all-things. Even under an overcast sky, it allowed us to see fifty yards down a trail.

We came down the mountain by a different trail and went back toward our intended campsite on the lower third of the eastern slope. Some of the trails were well traveled, but the one we were on should not have been. We were surprised not only to see tire tracks on it but to see such deep, heavy ones. I knelt and felt the track, Rick did the same. In daylight, we could have been sure of the time the tracks were made, but the thaw and refreezing had mottled the track in a way it would take a lot of good light to read. My guess was a week; in the light I would have been sure.

It was strange to see a heavy car like a Buick back that far in the woods, and we followed the tire marks to right near where we were going to camp. We could see were the car started and stopped, but the tracks of the people who had gotten out of it were too jumbled to read in the dark. We walked over to a partly cleared spot and brushed it clean for our campfire. After we had a fire going, Rick and I sat and drank a cup of coffee and looked at the stars.

"Know any good Jersey Devil stories?" he said. He knew every story I knew and we had told each other hundreds of them sitting on the edge of the cedar swamp waiting for the fire to die down sufficiently to make shadows real. Each story was about a huge, hairy creature like Big Foot but with a bad disposition. "Hundreds,'' I said. Rick looked at me with a challenging smile. I believe his mood had given him that uneasiness earlier, and he wanted to reassure himself that we were really beyond any childish things like fear of things that have no real power to harm.

"How about the mud one?" he said. It was our favorite. I could quote the story by heart then and often did. I wove a long introduction to the story, telling who the people involved were. I did a long thing on the background of a man named McDaniels who was building a hunting cabin in the deep pines with his son.

At the end I quoted his son. "My father went down to the edge of the muddy bank of the swamp to draw some water. I saw his silhouette near the edge as it was just about dark. Then I stood there, scared to death, as another shape appeared from the mud, grabbed my father and pulled him under. The mud was all covered with blood.''

Rick smiled across the campfire. It was hotter than we needed, the ground around it was beginning to thaw and a circle immediately next to the fire was drying out. "You think that's true?"

I wasn't entirely sure, but I believed there was *something* to it. "What else could it be?" I said and Rick shrugged.

"I don't know," he said, "maybe somebody wanted to kill him.''

I thought about that for a while. "He must have been a great stalker," I said. Rick wanted to know who was a great stalker and I said, "The guy who murdered McDaniels, if it wasn't the Jersey Devil." Rick's eyes lit up. We could see the man watching McDaniels for weeks, getting his routine down. We reconstructed how it would have been done. The man must have hidden in the swamp all day and then lay down on his back in the mud just before McDaniels came down.

"He must have grabbed McDaniels when he bent down for the water and stabbed him," Rick said.

The excitement of figuring it out ran through me.

"Then when McDaniels jerked back up he pulled the guy with him."

Rick was nodding furiously. "Yeah, and then he must have stabbed him in close, pulled him back down, and crawled away dragging the body." I had a picture of a creature bigger than a man buried, all but his eyes, in the soft mud, springing up out of it, and tearing at the man with his teeth. But I could not make the picture credible as I once would have been able to. I had outgrown that long before; we both had, but it was the first time we had reasoned sceptically into the myth we had had so much fun scaring each other with. "What do you suppose he killed him for?" I said. Rick shrugged, annoyed that we had established the method to his satisfaction and there was no use speculating on the causes. "He must have hated him an awful lot," I said.

Rick started to say something but a gust of wind caught the fire and fanned it to twice its size. Rick jumped back, slapping at the scorch smouldering on his jacket sleeve. The wind blew the fire back away from us with equal ferocity and then died. Rick settled back and took up his coffee cup.

I suppose he didn't see it at first because he was looking down into his cup, but I sat with mixed fascination and horror as the ground parted slowly a foot or so beyond the flames and, inch by inch as if it were fighting against itself, a human hand emerged from the ground.

All I could think of was it reaching out and grabbing us to drag us down into the ground, the Jersey Devil striking back at non-believers. I was frozen where I sat. It was not the hand, it was not the fact that it was human. It was not even the fact that it was clearly dead. It was the fact that it was popping up out of the ground that left me speechless with curiosity and terror.

Rick sat back as the palm broke through the surface. He watched it rise up until it was almost vertical, the fingers spread and clawed, all the muscles pulled tight by the stiffening of death, and dusted with cold to a whitish blue tinge. Rick watched it rise to its most upright point and stop, its bent fingers spread out like the branches of a little tree. He looked down into his cup and swirled the last of the coffee around in the bottom and drank it. He turned his cup upside down and let the last drop fall to the ground, then he reached over and hung the cup on the extended thumb.

"It's getting a little crowded around here," he said, "I think we ought to move." I was already breaking camp. In an hour we had cleared the area of our camp-fire and everything we could imagine anyone finding as evidence that we had been there. We took our packs and moved our camp five miles east. On the way, we decided that the body was another mob execution, and we argued whether or not we should report it and face the mob's wrath. The real problem, of course, was not the mob but our parents. They would believe that there were bodies rising up out of the ground every ten feet and murders every twenty. By the time they were finished thinking about it, Rick and I would have been tethered close to home for a month or so until we could convince them otherwise. We agreed on an anonymous phone call to the police.

It was a two mile walk to the telephone at the general store. The police wanted us to come in and lead them there, but we gave them directions and hung up. The police were also the firemen in those days, and they knew the trails well enough to find the body without us. In an hour, they would have a full crew of people out there investigating. We agreed it was a perfect op-portunity to practice our stalking, and we hiked back to the mountain and came in from the far side of our campsite.

The sky had cleared, and the stars were bright and firm. Our fear had spent itself and only curiosity remained. It was a difficult stalk; the cold made everything crackle, and we had to move very slowly the last hundred yards or so until we were invisibly set just beyond the circle of their lights. They had just begun to dig up the body, and we listened to them speculate on whether or not the callers had had anything to do with the murder. One of the cops said "Naw, it was only kids, scared to death. Probably home in bed now."

I didn't look at Rick because I would have burst out laughing. The other man was not convinced, "Well what the hell would kids be doing out here in the middle of the night?" The cop had no answer for that at first, but he decided that we had come out in the late afternoon and found it and had been too scared to call until later.

The body was out by then, and somebody called over that it had been shot through the head, one time, behind the right ear. Somebody offered the obvious, that it was a mob execution. Somebody else insisted that it was the car with the New York license plates that had been around for a few hours a week or so before.

The medical examiner confirmed that the body was probably in the ground for a week, although the freeze made it difficult to tell. Rigor mortis, he said, had forced the hand up through the sand as the campfire had thawed the ground. We waited for them to carry the corpse out to the body carrier and leave. But they seemed as full of curiosity as we were, and one of them suggested that they get the dogs and search the area.

It was a ridiculous idea; the scent was more than a week old, it was a cold night, keeping odors close to the ground, and the body would have distracted all but the best trained dogs, which these clearly weren't.

The men moved around in front of the headlights like aliens silhouetted in the glare. The contrast of light and dark made them look like huge, shambling creatures, and for a second I had the vision that we were watching a whole family of Jersey Devils out for a picnic. I wanted to tell Rick that, but we were too close for conversation, and the dogs were out of the car by then. We moved ten feet further back into the woods and sat confidently.

The dogs were ordinary house dogs rather than bloodhounds, and the cold made our scent lie heavy and close to the ground. Two of the dogs were too young even to hunt, and the other two did not seem to have the talent to pick up a difficult scent. We might have slipped away then, rather than risk them stumbling on us by accident, but the first of them had started toward us, and motion would have made us visible.

There were too many scents for an untrained dog to pick up, and they ran around in confused circles until they blundered near us. I had an impulse to bolt, but I knew from the deer that standing still was almost as good as being invisible. Many times Rick and I had crouched motionless at the side of a well-traveled trail and watched people go right past us without noticing. One of the older dogs came right for me, and I reminded myself that we were invisible to the animals, and that he would not see me. Years later a similar thing happened when I was tracking an armed robbery suspect. But the stakes were different then. At fourteen, I would rather have been shot than be kept from coming into the Pine Barrens for the rest of my life.

I froze, and stilled my breathing. The dog came up along the tree I was crouched against and sniffed it. When he lifted his leg to mark it, I could have reached out and startled him. When he put his head down to sniff again, I could have pulled his tail and maybe sent him chasing it. I almost had to sit on my hands not to do it, and it was all Rick could do not to stand up and tell them that if they gave us some light over on the tracks, we could tell them who did what and when. But we stayed where we were, and the dogs caught the scent of a squirrel or something and bounded off into the woods. Half the party had to go and round them up, and in the confusion we slipped easily away.

We stayed up for a while when we got back to camp, trying to figure out how anybody could use a place as beautiful as the Pine Barrens to murder someone in. Or why they would spread litter everywhere they went, or why anybody would dump their garbage in a place as sacred as the Pine Barrens. More than anything that night we wanted to drive from the Pine Barrens and from the face of the earth all those shadowy people hiding something deep in the woods. I believe that what happened when I met the poachers was a direct result of that night.

We watched the sun come up, a white-yellow hole behind the fog, pointing where night had gone. Then we slept for a while and packed our gear and went home, swearing to our parents that the night had been short and the woods empty and we had seen nothing at all.

FOREFOOT

HIND FOOT

BOBCAT· OUR BEST PLASTER CAST

15/The End of the World

*All week we had lived in Rick's backyard, our parents'
mercy in the face of the inevitable. Rick's leaving
seemed unreal, and we had enjoyed the packing. But it
had come time to look our loss in the face and accept it.
I was no good at that.*

Everywhere I looked, everywhere I walked, something I
had shared with Rick would be there. It was impossible
to think of the woods without him, even though I had
been there alone time and again. The times we were
apart we shared when we got together again. I wondered
who I would share all the triumphs and treasures of the
day with once Rick was gone. I wondered who would
understand how much time and effort a skull cost. Who
would appreciate the patience and brilliant deduction

that turned a skull into a creature. I wondered who would care.

But I said nothing about what I wondered. We both said we would write. I gave Rick my address even though he knew it as well as his own, and he promised to send me his as soon as he found out what it was. We left the hard things unsaid. I knew him better than anyone in the world. He had shared my life. There was nothing that could replace that. And nothing could change the fact that he was leaving. That fact came between us whenever anyone opened his mouth, and we spoke in awkward formal phrases that muffled the grief. It was as if we had become the strangers that lifelong friends turn into when they come home from separate colleges. Nothing could be adequately said between us.

And yet we tried to say it. Over and over. But there was nothing to say that wouldn't make the going even harder, so we stuck to the meaningless. At times we just let the conversation lapse into a silence that was deeper than absence. When the silence got unbearable, I took out the skull I knew Rick had always wanted. I started to say that I wanted him to have it to remember me by, but it sounded dumb. Everything sounded dumb when I thought it, and what we said sounded dumber still. Finally I thrust the skull at him as if I wanted him to take it away before I had to explain it.

He took the skull and smiled. It was the snapping turtle skull he had always wanted. "It's the snapping turtle skull you always liked," I said. It sounded so incredibly obvious. I felt like an idiot. Rick smiled and nodded as if the explanation had really been necessary. He didn't look at me for a while, he just kept turning the skull over and over in his hands. I must have known that he was sitting there fighting back the tears that grown men and Indians are not allowed. But I could not admit that to myself and still keep up the facade, so I swung back in my chair and stared at the floor.

Eventually Rick got up and went to his jacket and came back with another skull wrapped in tissue. He held it out to me, and I took it with a solemnity that was

foolish and tragic all at the same time. We stuffed formality between us so the space wouldn't look so empty.
I unwrapped the skull delicately and looked. It was the
skull I knew it could be, the cat I had eyed so often. It
was Rick's best skull, just as my gift to him had been my
best. But there was no way to acknowledge it, except
with a long swallow and a nod.

We sat a long time fingering our skulls, examining
them as if we had not seen them hundred of times
before. I think one of us mumbled thanks. I said, "I,
uh, guess we ought to do the tracks." He nodded. The
past was easier to think about than the future.

"They're up in the closet," I said. It was redundant.
He had helped me get them down a thousand times,
sliding the big box off the top shelf as if the fragile
plaster tracks broke like soap bubbles from the touch.
We had been making plaster casts of tracks for years,
and the improvement in our skills was evident as we
went through them each time.

I couldn't think of them without thinking of the
hours we had spent crouching over the slowly drying
plaster, pouring it slowly into the track, careful not to
bruise the peaks. Each cast was a masterpiece of
concentration and skill, guarded against chips and
scratches, cleaned and taken care of. Every one of them
represented some amazing incident, some remarkable
sight, some trip, some exploration. Together they
formed the trail of our life in the woods, each print ad-
vancing a step in time.

The most important times in my life lay in that old
cardboard box on the top shelf of my closet preserved in
plaster of Paris. The best times in Rick's life were there
too and we both knew it. That was how I knew
inescapably that we were at the end of our trail together.
It had come time to divide up our joint past like a
husband and wife dividing up their children. Yet I had
no desire to keep them all. What Rick took would be
mine as well, and there were a lot of incidents that I
wanted him to take with him.

It was impossible in a way, the dividing up of our

past, and we both knew it. "Yeah," he said. "We should get them down and look at them at least." But neither of us moved to do it. Maybe we knew that we couldn't look at them without all that we were holding back bubbling over. Or perhaps we waited because it was such a final act, dividing up the memories because there wouldn't be any more. Maybe we knew how the letters would dwindle and finally stop altogether after a year. Probably, we knew how little they would say. People with different lives were different people. Time and distance would make us strangers.

The next night there would be some solace. Stalking Wolf, Rick, and I would go to the Good Medicine Cabin for one last time. In the timelessness of the Pine Barrens it would seem, for a few hours, as if we were beyond the calls of duty and family. Stalking Wolf would talk to us, and his hand would rise and give us a certainty that we would meet again, in this world or the next.

He would tell me that the forest was still mine, that I had experienced it alone from the beginning, just as Rick had experienced it alone, because the forest talks to everyone in a different way and what it says to one is never quite what it says to another. The next night, Stalking Wolf would tell me that I would find it hard for a while to be separated from my blood brothers, but that I would turn back to the forest and be at one with it again. His hand would move and grasp and paint the world as it would be without Rick or Stalking Wolf, and I would see in its motion the fatal inevitability. The hand would go out in front of him like a separate vision of the world and smooth down the years with the promise that we would meet again. The hand would fist and palm and knuckle the last consolation, that we were brothers by blood and by choice, and could never truly be separated.

But the soothing eloquence of Stalking Wolf's hand was in the future, the temporary anesthetic of his words were hours too far ahead to do either of us any good. We sat in my room with the silence between us like a deep, unbroken snow. It was the first time there had ever been silence *between* us. We had reached that point where there was everything to say and no way for men to say it. There was nothing left to do but get down the box.

It was high on the shelf and every time we took it down was an adventure. Every safe return was an adventure ended. The exchange was a delight of teamwork. I stood on a chair and reached up to grab its edge. Rick waited for me to start to pass it down. The box was big and bulky, but we were confident; any time it had ever begun to fall, one pair of hands or the other was there to catch it almost before it even began to move.

I slid the box off the shelf and started to pass it down. I don't know how it dropped. At 11:00 the next night, we would leave the Pine Barrens for the last time together. At 4:00 A.M. both Rick and Stalking Wolf would be gone. I don't know how the box fell. Maybe we had moved apart already and couldn't judge the distances between us any more. Maybe there would have been too many unbearable memories if it had been taken down safely to the bed. In any case, it fell.

I knew by the sound that nothing would survive the crash. The box hit and bounced open, scattering pieces of plaster across the floor. The carefully wrapped tissue did nothing to protect. The cardboard box only spread the impact evenly. Everything was gone. Every single piece was broken beyond repair. There was no need even to open it to be sure; almost ten years of work had been obliterated in an instant. I came down slowly. Rick stood without saying anything. Carefully I lifted the box away from the pile that spilled out beneath it. There was nothing left that could be salvaged. Our past lay in pieces all around us.

I don't know why we started to laugh. Maybe it was because we didn't have to talk about it now. Maybe it was the irony of having such a heavy task taken from us so sharply. Maybe it was the irony of *all* the pieces breaking at once. Maybe it was the sudden unexpected release of tension. Or maybe, we laughed so hard and long, because we were too old to cry.

WHITE-TAILED DEER LEAPING IN WET SAND

16/Guardian

The grief of Rick's leaving stayed with me for a long time. I brooded on it. I wandered in the fog of my loneliness for weeks, missing half of what I saw, not appreciating the rest because Rick was not there to share it. For a while, I went into a decline, even though Stalking Wolf was right. The forest was still as beautiful and variable as it had always been, but there was a bittersweet tinge to seeing the Barn Swallows take their flying circus through the clearing knowing Rick was not there to see it also. And the joy I felt coming across a nest of baby rabbits in the wet grass turned to ash when I realized that there was no one to tell about it.

Several times I started down a track with the old elation of being on the trail of some natural mystery, only to lose interest after a few hundred feet. I spent long hours just staring at the pines and the clouds, wondering what Rick was doing and if I would ever see old grandfather Stalking Wolf again. Spring had ripened. There were more birds than I could count, but I barely saw them. Even George and Alice, the cardinals who lived near the Good Medicine Cabin, only made me feel sad when I saw them. I envied them, still together sharing everything they did, as they would until one of them died, while the only other members of my species who would understand my song were gone forever.

I moved through the woods like a ghost, wandering without purpose or attention. I made my camps mechanically, ate little, slept more than I was used to. Only the most amazing sights could rouse me out of my lethargy. A great apathy overcame me. I believe there is a point where grief turns inward and becomes despair or turns outward and becomes rage. Which way it goes depends on the catalyst. I was sinking deeper into self-pity and depression, and it took an almost unspeakable horror to turn me around.

I didn't see the deer at first coming through the swamp. I was almost on top of him when he bolted, a huge Virginia White-tail that crashed away from me through the cedars like a runaway truck. For the first time in days, I felt an interest in the world again. I watched him break through the branches in blind panic beyond the swamp into the trees. It would be an easy track, and as I followed it, it did not absorb me enough to keep back the depression I had been fighting ever since Rick and Stalking Wolf had left. It crept over me, trying to turn me aside to some stump where I could brood the day away. But I followed the trail anyway, even though my mind wandered to things Rick and I had seen or done, and to the guidance and understanding I would no longer be able to get from grandfather Stalking Wolf. When I came into the clearing, I almost did not notice the slaughtered deer.

Only when the tracks of the Virginia buck startled and leapt to its right, did I look to see what could have sent it leaping away in terror. What I saw sickened and disgusted me. There were three carcasses of what had once been deer, all of them sliced cleanly through the hind quarters and broken apart at the shoulders. I stood stunned at the waste.

Only some poacher from the city would butcher a deer for the hindquarters and the shoulders. Those parts brought a fair price in New York. The rest of the deer was not worth caring about and they had left the half mutilated bodies lie where they butchered them like bent beer cans littered in the grass. The sparse grass of the clearing was full of dried blood, and gallons of it seemed to have soaked into the sand, staining it permanently. I felt as if someone had kicked me in the stomach.

The tire track of a pick-up truck went away from the slaughter toward a road and I followed them without thinking. I don't remember how far I went before the tracks veered off into the woods again, but I remember steeling myself for what I would find where the tracks stopped again. The overlap of the outgoing tracks told me I would find another bloodbath, but I lied to myself that it might only be a place where the poachers had picked up less successful butchers. The second sight was worse than the first.

Six deer seemed to have been sawed in half and their forelegs cut out at the shoulder from the halves of the bodies that remained. I tried to look away. I had cleaned and dressed deer myself; it was a necessity and I could find, if not a beauty, at least a fascination in the intricate workings of the deer's body that had labored so long to bring me meat. But there was ferocity to the butchering, a quality of sadistic delight, that had splashed the blood around on the trees, and on the grass. There was a wide, dark puddle soaking into the sand where half a deer must have lain over the tailgate dripping. Their backs looked like someone had come down through them with a chain saw. Everything was blood and hair. Everywhere I looked the footprints whirled in an orgy of slashing and breaking. Ripped sinews hung like untied shoelaces. Veins had little clotted caps. Fur was matted, thick and useless. I turned away in disgust, and followed the tracks.

I found two more places where the hunting parties had dragged the carcasses to a central point and cut them apart before I found the truck. The blood at the last place was still fresh. I touched a drop of it hanging from a blade of grass like some perverted dew. It seemed sticky and unclean and I felt defiled to be seeing it.

I could not look closely at the last deer; they were butchered more hurriedly and more brutally than the others. No doubt the poachers were in a hurry to get back to the cards and beer. One of the carcasses was a doe. Someone had thrown the foetus up against a tree.

I staggered out of the clearing and down the tracks of the truck that bit heavier into the sand under its load. I found it only a few miles further on. The carcasses were tossed in the back like broken logs, stiff and ugly in their death. I wondered how something so agile, so graceful in the flowing motion of its stride, could be reduced to so much carrion. I knew where their headquarters would be.

There was an old cinder block railroad shed a quarter of a mile away. It had been built long before out of the old-fashioned cinder blocks made with big cinders. The wind had pounded some of them completely apart leaving hand-sized gaps in the walls. The blocks that remained were more like brittle slabs of crust that had dried in place.

They had left the truck far enough from camp to leave themselves some escape time if anyone found it. I came up on the back of the windowless shed, but I could see movement through the chinks and gaps in the cinder block and in the cracks where the cheap cement had gone dry, cracked, and fallen out. I started around the side of the shed toward the only door, but fragments of fur and blood near the corner stopped me.

Someone had blown a squirrel apart, at close range, probably for fun. A big pine tree near the corner of the shed had the marks of a knife being thrown and retrieved repeatedly, and beyond it was the last of the deer hung by its heels to drain. It turned slowly on the rope, and when its eye fastened on me I felt for a moment as if it was not merely a deer but one of the deer that had given us the gift of their motion as they came bounding through our camp at the Good Medicine Grounds.

I felt so ashamed of myself that I leaned against the wall and began to cry. If I had been more alert, if I had not shut myself off from the flow of nature, I would have known something was wrong in the woods. If I had not allowed myself to be blinded by my grief, I would have noticed earlier the small signs of the poachers' passage. I had let my gifts decay. I had, in feeling sorry for myself, abandoned my duty to the woods and to the animals. The Good Medicine Deer hung by its heels, bleeding for my foolishness, dead from my apathy. All my grief for the slaughtered, for Rick and Stalking Wolf gone, for the Good Medicine Deer chopped and packaged, rushed out of me in broken sobs.

And as it went, it left a vacuum that drew in the rage.

It has taken me years to remember exactly what I did, and even now it's vague, as if someone else did it all and I stood aloof from it somehow. But the rage that filled me was only partly my own, and the vengeance was no more mine than the bite of the Guardians was theirs. I felt some force larger than myself take possession of me, and I believe it was not my strength alone, nor the long hours of training, of kicks and punches done a thousand times until the whole force of the body comes into focus at the precise point of impact, that caved in the wall in front of me.

I clenched my fists, and as my breath rushed in, I filled with a power, terrible and implacable. I spun with a screaming shout that rang in my own ears like the cry of some enraged and wounded animal. The muscles of my thigh bunched and straightened and my heel slammed against the crumbling wall. On the second kick, a section of wall as big as a man crashed inward like the slamming of a gigantic door. As the four men inside stood open-mouthed waiting to see what would come flying through the hole, I turned the corner of the shed toward the front door.

They had hung a sheet across the open doorway, even though it was warm spring, and a man was sitting against it cocked back in a chair. He was halfway to his feet when I grabbed him and threw him through the doorway. He felt no heavier than a chair in my hands, and he broke against the far wall and slid to the floor.

Rage whirled me into the room. Two men sat behind a table against the rear wall, and I went for them like a wild dog going for the jugular. The table split like kindling, and I threw the pieces of it aside. The men sat petrified. Somewhere outside someone was screaming that there was a crazy man inside killing everybody. He begged somebody to help him, but the law was as absent for him as it had been for the deer.

I went for the wall behind and to the side of the men and kicked and kicked at it until four of the weakest blocks disintegrated and a huge section of it flew outward. One of the men jumped up and broke for the door, but I grabbed him by the arm and swung him in a circle until he crashed out through the hole in the wall and lay groaning outside. All the time I was roaring and screaming, "You killed my deer! You killed my deer!"

Then I went across to the front wall and began kicking at it until it flew out also in a shower of cinders. The other man still sat by the table wide-eyed with horror. I grabbed him by the throat and crotch and rammed him headfirst into the other wall. He crumpled and I stood him up against the wall holding him by the shirt front. My rage wanted to kill him, but even the horror I had seen did not justify it, and I let the punch that should have killed him go past his head and into the wall.

I believe I was crazy at that moment, and for an instant, the craziness almost made me a murderer. My fist cocked, full of lethal justice, and slammed forward. But it turned aside at the last instant and crashed into the wall. I hit the wall again to keep from killing him, and I kept on punching the cinder block beside his head and shouting incoherently at him.

The cinder block kept sputtering fragments of stone back at me and chips of it dusted my shoulder. I don't think he was entirely conscious, but I kept warning him and punching and punching away at the cinderblock beside his head until it crumbled. Then I spun him around and flung him out through the hole in the front wall.

The last of the four men inside the shed was against the far wall trying to load a shotgun. Sunlight came through in slits between the cinder blocks behind him and fanned out past him. Dust swirled up in it like fire. I yanked the gun from his hands and smashed it against the wall. It came apart in my hands. The man ran screaming for the front door as I grabbed a second gun and bent the barrel across my knee. Then I flung it out through the back wall and started kicking the walls again until the last solid section flew out and the wall caved in.

The roof came swinging down with a groan and stopped a few feet from the floor. I kicked out one last brittle section of wall and walked out through the front doorway. The man I had thrown out through the front wall lay moaning near the hole. When he saw me he tried to crawl away screaming, "Don't kill me! Don't kill me!" I turned to say something to him but all that came out was a hideous strangled growl, and I wondered for a moment if the Jersey Devil wasn't just a series of ordinary people nature took into her hands like a set of tools.

The last man was running down one of two converging roads yelling for help. I turned and went back the way I had come, tearing the branches off trees as I went and uprooting bushes and throwing them out of the way like some huge animal emptying the last of its rage. Behind me, the camp looked like a battlefield filled with wounded crying for help, or simply crying. When I came to the truck, the rage almost started back up to full intensity, and I tore a piece off my shirt and stuffed it into the gas tank. I lit the tail that hung back out and walked away.

My hands were swollen and bloody, and there was blood down my arms, and some of it was smeared across my chest. My hands were clawed, but I had no reason to open them. My knuckles were flattened and displaced, and there was a long scrape down one forearm like the ragged edge of a cinder block had been dragged across it.

I walked down the road in a daze. I barely heard the roar of the exploding truck. I simply shuffled forward with no place to go and no place behind me, until the first of the fire trucks came roaring past. I barely noticed it, but I heard the second one coming and turned off into the woods that seemed suddenly clean and bright and new.

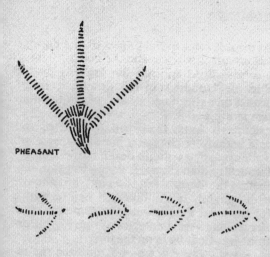

PHEASANT

17/Thoreau Summer

I sat naked in the warm rain of my eighteenth summer watching the storm that had begun more than a day before. I had not moved very much, and I had taken my eyes off the sky only intermittently to watch the way the land reacted to the changes above it. From time to time, I glanced at my own bare footprint deteriorating in the rain. I had seen that process unfold a thousand times, but it never failed to fascinate me. The steady drop by drop erosion of the track was different each time, and I learned an unappreciated nuance or a new insight every time I watched it.

I had watched the storm in the same way, backtracking it down the sky. The high, wispy fingers of cloud stretched down the long incline of the cold front to a bunched shoulder like an arm reaching through a slot into the unknown. I watched the fingers of cloud grope above me, fasten somewhere beyond the horizon behind my head and begin to drag itself ponderously up the ramp of colder air. Hundreds of miles away, stacks of clouds separated one after another and began to climb the line of temperature.

Hour by hour the clouds thickened and fluffed and darkened, and with every change in the sky, the colors in the pines changed. The wildlife began to move faster and more frequently, like shoppers trying to get in one last errand before the storm. I felt the wind shift and the pine needles lift slightly in the breeze. I had to wait a long time for the great thunderheads to come towering across the sky trailing wispy tentacles of rain like a Portuguese man-o'-war floating in on the tide.

Bit by bit, the sky came down and squeezed the invisible layer between it and the earth; the trees and bushes bunched and sprawled accordingly. The wind became a loud voice announcing the coming of a greater power. Animals huddled as if the angel of death were passing over, but to me there was only magnificence. The crackle of lightning lit the sky out of its noontime dark, and the rain came down like a message of unsolvable complexity. The clouds rumbled silently overhead thinning gradually into sunlight that dried everything except the deeper puddles.

For two months I had been living outside of time watching the Pine Barrens dance toward fall. My days had no names, hours were meaningless. Some shift in the season would tell me when it was time to go. In the meantime, I roamed invisible in the deepest part of the forest. I ate when I was hungry, if at all, or nibbled as I went on berries and roots. Sometimes I ate a snapping turtle or a fish in a fine soup of sparkling Pine Barrens water and herbs. At times, I believe I went foodless for days without noticing.

I slept between experiences, sometimes in the day, sometimes at night, whenever I couldn't stay awake any longer or when one irresistible mystery was temporarily solved and the next had not yet begun. But there was so much to see and do that I doubt that I slept much more than I ate. And yet I had gained weight and felt stronger and more rested than at any time in my life before or since.

It took weeks to disentangle myself from the pattern of the world, but I had begun in early spring, and by the time unofficial summer came, I had lost my sense of time and obligation. I had my knife, and the Pine Barrens gave me everything else I needed. For amusement, I had a sky full of fascinating riddles moving whole nations of animals through the intricate patterns of their daily life. For enlightenment, I had the question of how.

I don't know exactly when I took off my clothes, but I believe it was early summer, though the whole season came and went so smoothly and so quickly that a day was indistinguishable from a week. But I remember it as a conscious act, a declaration of freedom. I did not put my clothes back on again all summer, except to watch the dogs.

They were my obsession for a time, and I studied them, crawling so close that if the wind changed direction they would have been on me before I could run. I watched the 140 dog pack coalesce and then separate, according to some canine logic, into foraging groups that went out from the dump for days at a time. I watched the hierarchy of bite and bluster work out its differences as dogs gained and lost their positions in the pack.

I saw the hard, older dogs break in the new ones, reteaching them the things civilization had taught them to forget. I watched the new dogs learn what their teeth were really for, and I listened to them practicing their growling in the dark. When they stayed in the dump, I watched them, and when they went out along the four looping runs that formed a propeller with the dump as its hub, I watched their trail. Only once did it lead out of the woods completely.

In the second week I watched them, four dogs broke from the pack unobtrusively, as if they were sneaking away to share some common secret. I followed them out of the dump and through the woods until they came to four houses set almost beside one another, where they fawned and begged and wagged their tails at masters who had no idea that they had even been gone. Near the houses, they were docile, friendly dogs that anyone could go up to and pet, but I could not go close to the house. I was not that kind of animal anymore, one that could live in the woods and still go home and beg for handouts. Months without the clock had made me a wild creature with no tolerance for civilized things.

The sight of houses made me nervous and when the people came out, opening the screen doors with one hand to set down a beggar's bowl of food, I had to look away to keep from being drawn back into that waking dream. I knew that whatever I did, I would never completely be a part of that tameness again. I might, when times got hard, drift back into the world my parents considered real, but in my depths, the only truth was the passing moment and its infinite variety.

When the four dogs came back, they were sniffed and surrounded like strangers, and I knew what the wild dogs were smelling, the groveling loss of substance that was the price of living easy off the machine. None of those dogs rose to first bite, or even fifth. They ran a little behind the rest, deferentially, as if they knew that they were only pretend dogs, some human being's *idea* of a dog.

But one or two other new recruits would stay when the summer ended and the foraging got hard and the winds cold. One in five would regain its heritage and become a true carnivore again. The rest would stay man-dogs, half creatures, with no sense of themselves or their proper place. Dogs of the interface, they would run the between-world, too adventurous for the lawn and a short chain but too humanized to make the break complete.

I think that of all the creatures I saw in the woods, those half-wild dogs were the least natural, their reflexes slowed by command, their senses dulled by the odor of machines and the apparatus of mankind. Nothing they did ever had the style of true dogs; they always seemed to be holding back, as if they thought the discovery of their clandestine life would cost them their pension. I was no longer like that. I had become animal in some important and irreversible ways.

All summer I went through the woods from special place to special place looking for tidemarks, places to measure from while I was gone. Although I would be there in the Pines all winter, I knew as I walked that it would be years before I saw the Pine Barrens again in summer. In a year, I would be on journeys to other places, taking what I had learned and pitting it against what I had not learned to see what would happen.

The woods had changed since I had started to come into them. Some oil roads had become macadam, and some trails had become major, if short, highways for people looking for adventure of one kind or another. There were tracks near the Good Medicine Cabin that summer, leading in from the easy access of the power line roads. Their illegal drinking interrupted by police patrols, half-tame people dove into the woods in their dilapidated old cars and cancerous trucks until the Township's lone police car went by.

Some of them, drunk or in blind flight, apparently got lost on the trails and then finally found their way back again. Probably they came back sober and tried to retrace their steps, learning new trails all the time. Perhaps one out of fifty of them might eventually get out of their truck and begin to explore on foot, gaining a reverence for the woods as they went. But most were looking for greater danger or a safer place to hide.

Stage by stage, I watched their tracks go from short, hesitant explorations of the major trails to highspeed search-and-destroy missions down otherwise trackless trails. Only one trail had the steady motion of someone who thinks, "It-all-comes-out-someplace, enjoy-the-ride." One set of tracks hinted at someone who might eventually come to understand the woods. I could read the drunkenness in the rest, leaping and wallowing downhill, skidding corners sloppily, crashing through mud puddles headlight high and tearing up half an acre of trees to throw under the wheels for traction. More than once I found half their load dropped in the dark along a staggering path of tracks and broken shrubs.

But their foolishness bothered me less than the familiarity I read in their tracks. The tracks had a boldness that comes only when an animal knows his territory well and is testing himself against it for the first time. I had seen new dogs stumble clumsily over the dumps until they learned to walk leaning into the slope. It always made them reckless when they first learned it. The intruders were the same. They knew a few square miles of road well. They drove them drunk. It was only a matter of time before they stopped for one reason or another and saw the cabin through the trees. I had to prevent that.

I held that ground sacred then, thinking my skill came from the place rather than the experience. It seemed to me that my survival was at stake, and yet I did not feel the rage that I had felt against the poachers, and I did not want violence. I went back to the tracks again and again as if by being there I could somehow keep them away from the cabin. If I could keep them from finding it until the first frost, it would be all right after that. The woods would be empty again until spring, and I would worry about spring when it came.

But there was nothing I could do to stop them, and I watched in helpless frustration as the tracks moved closer and closer to the cabin. I needed the Good Medicine Cabin; I needed to take its image with me intact when I left the pines.

All summer I wandered down from time to time to watch the tracks creep closer like a gently rising tide. I must have become obsessed with the idea because I would find a track, just missing some point from which they could see the cabin, and I would hurry back to check it again a few days later only to find that the track was only a few hours older than before. I cursed them for bringing time back into my life.

My days had sequence but not chronology. I could remember the sequence of weather for days back, but night and day were only facets of the unceasing flow of weather around and over me. I could not have given any day but the first a date or a name, and I do not know when I first became aware of the tracks as a danger. But I knew that there was always danger when carnivores met in the woods and that man is the most dangerous carnivore of all.

What happens when carnivores confront is governed by the necessity to survive. The initial response of a carnivore to surprise is flight, since those who underestimate the danger of the unknown tend to perish oftener than those who overestimate it. Most animals flee unless they are sure at a glance that the odds are heavily in their favor. A species that attacked automatically instead of preparing to flee would have to have an extremely low population in a given region or it would kill itself off as members of the species kept running into and attacking one another. Thus, most animals will flee if startled, and the vast majority of animals will avoid a confrontation with man if they have a clear escape route. Except in cases where abandoning the field threatens the survival of the animal more than staying, an animal will run rather than attack. When the pack got hungry, it was a lot harder for the Alpha dog to drive a less aggressive dog off his share of the food, and once while I watched, he had to savage one of the newer dogs for not backing off quickly enough.

However, when you corner an animal, especially if you come upon it suddenly, cutting off its only escape route, it will attack. Biological imperatives drive it to attack. How close you must come depends on the animal, but there is a point for every species past which all action is interpreted as an overwhelming threat, and the only response is ATTACK!!

Having once cornered an animal and escaped without injury, only a fool would pursue it and corner it again. Even the normally timid rabbit will attack when there is no other avenue of action. Every animal has a point where it will turn and fight because it sees that further flight is impossible and death is the obvious alternative. Only a very hungry predator takes its prey when the prey has turned instead of while it's on the run. A fleeing animal is a vulnerable animal. A trapped animal has nothing else to lose. And sometimes, the unexpectedness of its ferocity creates enough space for it to escape. The cornered attack is a last chance, however unlikely, at survival.

All summer the tire tracks backed me into a corner at the Good Medicine Cabin. It was a sacred place. I did not know then that an omen is preserved in the spirit, and I believed that the Good Medicine Cabin was the omen itself instead of being simply the place where the omen had occurred. I had become invisible there. The magical deer had flowed from the woods there, weaving me forever into the pattern of the Pine Barrens. They could not be abandoned. Confrontation became inevitable. Even my dreams told me so.

It was not always the same dream at first, but it was always similar, and it came to me off and on throughout the summer until it finally worked itself into a permanent version that came back two nights in a row before it drove me down to the Good Medicine Cabin. In the dream, three men got out of their jeep and came into the clearing where the cabin was. They were drunk, and they started to kick the cabin down, but it wouldn't go down because I was inside holding it up. They got thirsty with effort and got more and more drunk, the harder they tried to kick it down. Then one of them threw a bottle up against it, and the cabin burst into flames. They burned the cabin to the ground with me inside it, dancing around it, white renegades pretending to be Indians to shift the blame. They laughed and threw their beer cans into the fire, and one of them staggered up to water the flames. He came so close that his clothes were smoking when he turned around half finished and staggered away. When the fire was done smouldering, they kicked the chars away, and I rose up out of the ashes like the Jersey Devil and ate them alive. Or at least I was always on my way to eating them alive when I woke up, sweating and thirsty.

I hated that dream, both the part where I was destroyed and the part where I was the destroyer. It was a bad medicine dream full of bad medicine death, useless death from which nothing can be learned and nothing taken. I had almost had a death like that once when kids opened fire on our camp from across the stream, not knowing we were there. We crawled, howling and cursing, into the underbrush while half spent bullets dug themselves into the trees. For weeks afterward I thought how uselessly we might have died.

I wanted a death that would be an omen to anyone who saw it. I wanted a spectacular death, full of final insights. I did not care if it was a painful death as long as it was one from which something could be taken. I wanted my last track to be the sign of a struggle. I wanted a death where the signs of my going would say to whoever read them that if there was nothing beyond life but the abyss, I had gone into it taking the best of myself with me in one joyous leap. I did not want a bad medicine death.

There were so many kinds of bad medicine death. Killed by boredom and the tiny, unconnected insignificance of civilized life that hits like a predator coming in from above and behind you, as silent as night except for a little muffled rattle of wings and, if you are lucky, an awareness of the last, bright instant of pain and pleasure. Cancer. Heart attack. Stroke. Emphysema. Any number of insults to the body that come striking down out of the air or the water like flashing jaws snapping at your face out of the bushes. Useless death. Bad medicine death. Killed by accident by drunken idiots having a piece of sadistic fun. To disappear without a trace, buried in some shallow grave and added to the list of victims of the Jersey Devil. In a way, it really was the Jersey Devil that pursued me, and it was the myth of the Jersey Devil that saved me in the end.

It happened just around the bend from the Good

Medicine Cabin. The tracks were startlingly close. Fresh tracks, not more than an hour old. They had the weave of someone driving just short of the dangerous side of drunk; going slowly, looking for landmarks or trying to establish ones for finding their way back. I knelt by the tracks in the shadow of the bank. It was a bright night, but I had to feel the tracks for a while until I could get my eyes dimmed down to the level where they matched the darkness of the bank and I could see more or less clearly.

One set of tracks overlapped the other. The ones going in were unsteady or cautious, moving at five or ten miles an hour, weaving slightly. It was the track a driver might make leaning forward over the steering wheel and looking out and up through the windshield from time to time. If I had followed it a while, I would have come to a small swerve or two where he took another drink from a passed bottle. Given a day to follow the trail both ways, more than a stone's throw in either direction, I would eventually have found the bottle, a crushed cigarette pack, or a mound of butts.

Just up the road, there would be skid marks and plumes of strewn gravel where drivers had changed and someone aggressive, almost to the point of craziness, had taken the wheel. The tracks went off around the bend on the wrong side of the road, gaining speed. I did not need to go down the trail to know that I would find branches snapped off all the way along like bent blades of grass, dirt kicked out of the wheelruts on every curve, and handfuls of gravel scattered where it shouldn't have been, lighter side down.

I reached into the shadow of the bank to feel for the divots of scattered stones. If they had gotten out of the truck where the tracks stopped and started, they could have seen the cabin. If there was one stone overturned anywhere on that bank I wanted to find it before I went blundering into them in the dark without surprise on my side. I knew that there was nothing more dangerous in the deep woods at night than a half drunk man outside the reach of any restraint except his anesthetized conscience and his power to destroy.

I had abandoned the knife days before to live in the woods with only what the woods gave me. It was a good, bountiful summer, and the Pine Barrens took care of me, sheltered me, fed me. I was better off without it. The violence of the poachers had soured me even on revenge, and I did not want to harm them as I might if cornered and armed.

I could feel a disturbance in the boulder field at the foot of the bank. I closed my eyes to heighten the sensation in my fingers, focusing the whole of my attention on what I felt. Something made me turn my head to the left. Even through my eyelids, the lights were suddenly blinding.

I opened my eyes and the headlights were a flare of unbearable light. The roar of the engine sounded like the growl of a dog up close to my face. I dove blindly into the underbrush, feeling for a place to hide until my sight came back. By the time the jeep screeched to a stop, I sat wrapped around a short pine, my heart pounding like a deer's, waiting for the hunters to go by. The limbs went back out over and around me and I was buried in the tree. I broke two branches to cover up the bare spots near my face, and waited.

I had been so long in the woods alone that it did not occur to me that they were human like myself, that I might reason with them, or threaten them, curse them out, or simply talk to them. It never occurred to me to have any conversation with them any more than it would have to a deer. They were the hunters, I was the hunted.

The jeep stopped exactly where I had come diving into the woods. I wrapped my arms tighter around the trunk and hugged closer to the tree, losing myself deeper in its branches. I heard a door bang open and somebody thunder out. I heard somebody else shout, "What the hell *was* it, you guys?!"

A gruffer voice said, "A naked guy. He jumped in the bushes right here." There was a laugh that sounded like alcohol and the clatter of somebody inept climbing out of a jeep. "You sure it wasn't the Jersey Devil?"

"Naw, it was a guy, I'm telling ya, and where there's a naked guy, there's got to be a naked broad." They milled around the jeep like a pack at the crossroads of two scents.

"Let's get her!" The voice was the bay of a dog that always charges out of the confusion, howling after a false trail. No one moved.

"What the hell are *you* worried about, you won't get her till last anyway." The voice was the gruff growl of the Alpha man.

The voice of the Beta man answered from the jeep out of the sound of things being tossed around. "Where's the goddam flashlight, Jimmy?"

One of them climbed up the side of the jeep and turned a spotlight into the woods above me. I could tell it was the clumsy one. The beam played erratically in the treetops as if he had somehow got it tangled in the branches. The Alpha voice barked, "He's not in the trees, asshole!"

There was a whimper in the answer. "Well, what are we chasing *him* for anyway?" The gruffer voice laughed like two stones being grated together. "*He'll* tell us where *she* is." He must have turned toward the woods because his voice got louder. "I'll cut him a new hole if he doesn't." I peeked out through the branches. The laugh was grittier than before; it sounded like two six-packs of warm beer poured into a moron and allowed to ferment. The voice sounded like an ax being slammed into a live tree out of boredom.

I could see them only as shifting flashes of darkness flitting through the headlights, but I could hear them perfectly, and I knew which was which by the way they came into the woods. The one called Jimmy came crashing in, knocking the branches out of his way or jerking them up over his head and out of his face at the last second. His feet came kicking through the tangle around his ankles.

Off to his left, I could hear the clumsy one start in, picking his way as he went, without a plan, following the lead of the other two. If either of them attacked, he would join in just to escape being the scapegoat if the attack failed. In better company, he might have gotten a lot out of the woods, but he was a danger at that moment, whatever his out-of-the-woods character.

Probably the Alpha man was all mouth out of the woods, but he would have to prove himself if they found me. He would have to use the knife he apparently talked so much about or admit being a coward, and there was too much alcohol in his voice for me to imagine him doing that. I heard the clumsy one stop and pick out a path and then stumbled down it a few feet before he stopped again. "C'mon," he whined, "he's probably leading us away from her. This is a waste of time."

The Alpha man grunted. "Naw," he said, "he probably pushed her into the woods ahead of him, that's why he was still on the road." He pushed branches aside and peered into the underbrush. "She's probably laying in here somewhere." He sounded like a poacher looking for a wounded doe.

The voice of the Beta man came out of the darkness to his left. "You sure you saw him?" There was a challenge in his voice. "Or are you jerking us around again?"

The answer was belligerent. "Naw, I didn't see him. It was the Jersey Devil." The laugh that followed it was not as confident as it wanted to sound. I could hear the clumsy one crackling twigs back toward the jeep. The Beta man was making short soft steps turing him back toward the trail. I thought for a minute that they were going to leave, but the knife-holder moved irresolutely forward. Voices alone followed him deeper into the woods. It had become a matter of not losing face now. "C'mon, you'll never find him in there, Jimmy." I could hear the Beta voice turning to go, and I almost lowered the two branches I held in front of my face.

But the Alpha man's answer made me keep them where they were. The animal panic that had held me had begun to dwindle. I could see my position as a man would see it. If I attacked, I could probably get all three of them. Surprise, darkness, and the woods were all on my side, but what had happened at the poacher's cabin fell across me like a restraining hand and I would have crouched there until they went away if the one with the knife hadn't stumbled into me.

He tried to kick his way through some brambles, cursed, lurched and fell forward into the tree. When he grabbed for a branch to steady himself, he caught my wrist. I jerked it back and he gave a shriek. My wrist came out of his grasp like an adult's hand being pulled free of a child's. I could feel the fear in his fingertips as they slid over my wrist. I had only a split second to take advantage of it and everything from that point on was reflex.

Had I paused for rationality, I would have come up out of the bushes, screaming threats and curses, or stayed where I was, afraid to risk the vulnerability of a naked man. But there was no time for rationality, and I knew intuitively that if I could turn their fear to panic, I could turn their attack into a rout. I rose shrieking from the bushes, hoping all those times jumping out at Rick had not been for nothing.

The knife man staggered backward. Two steps back, he got momentary control of his flight and slashed out with the knife at one of the branches I had broken off to shield myself with. The branches extended my arms by a foot and must have made me look like some deformed creature reaching out of legend for a bloody mouthful.

Probably I could have come up screaming "Apple Pie!" and it would have worked. Everything was in my favor. I was coming out of nowhere at a man in a vulnerable position. I was startling him. His natural reaction would be to flee. Two quick strokes with the branches knocked the flashlight out of his hand and sent him toppling backward over a small pine. The spotlight played directly at me for a second, but there were half a dozen trees in the way and, if anything, the light must have made me look even more unreal. The pine needles that had stuck to my sweaty body gave me a coat of hair all over, and the ones I had stuck in my hair and beard for camouflage made me look like The One True Jersey Devil. The branches completed the picture with hairy lower arms and hands big enough to tear an ox in half.

The Alpha man rolled backward over himself and ran shrieking for the jeep. The Beta man turned and ran with his flashlight pointing down in front of his running feet. Almost out of the woods, he stopped and shined the flashlight back at me. I liked that trait, that not being able to wait until he was safe, to see what incredible thing was after him. It was something Rick would have done. I waved the branches in front of my face and leapt toward him.

He took a few steps away and turned again. I had grabbed the fallen flashlight by that time and as he turned back again, I held it pointing upward under my chin and made a face that would have made children laugh in other circumstances. But it was enough to give his panic something concrete to feed on, and he ran shouting for the jeep. I let out one of the long, wailing growls that Rick and I used to scare each other with in the cedar swamp as they fought their way over each other into the jeep.

They stalled out the jeep and I stood there praying for them to get it going again before they calmed down and saw only a nude man waving pine branches at them instead of the Jersey Devil. Finally, they got it going, and I leaped up again and gave another bloodcurdling howl. The jeep dug up fifty feet of trail as it went streaking away into the dark.

I stood in the silence watching where they had been. The blind animal panic I had felt was gone, but in its place was an equally animal exuberance that left me howling for the sheer pleasure of it long after they were out of earshot.

It seemed to turn suddenly cold when I stopped, and when I laughed I knew I had become human again. I could smell the coming of winter in the air. The next day, I put on my clothes and came out of the woods. It was a long time before I went back again in summer.

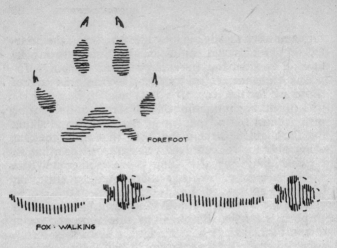

FOREFOOT

FOX · WALKING

18/Journeyman

Apprenticeship was hard. Journeymanship was long. Stalking Wolf trained us for four years, the last two of which were intense enough to be a full-time occupation, before we came of age and passed from apprentice to journeyman. But there were two stages to journeymanship; in the first, the journeyman is really an elevated apprentice. He is given more and more knowledge, but he uses it under the gradually loosening supervision of the master of the art.

Eventually, however, the journeyman must truly become the man who goes on journeys. The journeys he goes on are not quite important enough for the master to go on, or they come up when the master is busier elsewhere and needs a good representative. But they are journeys nevertheless, and while on them, the journeyman is on his own, limited in what he can do only by his skill and daring. There is not much practical difference between an independent journeyman and a master of the art.

I stopped being an apprentice at twelve, and I became an independent journeyman at sixteen when Stalking Wolf left. By eighteen, it had become clear to me that although there were countless things worth learning in the Pine Barrens, I was going to have to go somewhere else to become a complete master of my craft. At eighteen, I began the first of several journeys that would take me to the Grand Tetons, the Dakota Badlands, and the Grand Canyon. What finally set me moving was a trail that I found on my eighteenth birthday.

I was walking through the woods and I came across a trail that was at least two months old. The ground had frozen and unfrozen to different degrees all December and January, but there was still a readable print left. The tracks were erratic, and I followed them in staggering, frenzied circles. The body was not far away. I found his gun about thirty feet further on. I lifted back the bushes and there was the body.

The next day I went back and followed his tracks back to a jeep with a broken fanbelt. His tracks were all around it, and I found the deeper heel mark where he had jumped down. I followed the earliest set of tracks around the car. At almost each corner of the car there were sideward ridges on the print as if he had stopped and looked around. He had apparently ridden the jeep in circles until it died.

Panic must have set in a long time before or he wouldn't have run the engine past where he overheated it. If he had gone in short, quarter bursts and coasted when he could, he might still have gotten out without a fan belt and without overheating. But he must have jumped out of the jeep and run around the car looking for something, anything, that would seem like a key to the way out. The tracks dug in at the toes in a sort of frenzied shuffle around the car, checking each new horizon for some way to escape. In his growing panic, he was still methodical, organized. Snap decisions killed him. It must have dawned on him, when the heat indicator went on, that pretty soon he was going to have to start walking through that wilderness, so vast and intricate, that he had been riding through all morning trying to get out.

I believe he did not start running until late morning because a prudent man would have sat still until he had some light to distinguish the trails by. If he had started running in the night, it might have been because he was feeling the first hints of the oncoming heart attack that finally killed him. But I don't think he did. If he started driving even *late* at night, he would probably have outrun his panic by late morning when the car finally broke completely.

But the man who jumped out of the car and ran around it looking for a way out was still in the throes of a growing panic. He did not just spring from the car and start running. He looked around, perhaps frantically, before he set out, and he had the presence of mind to take his gun. He had come there to hunt, and it was probably in his mind that there were things in the woods, wild dogs at least, that might be hunting him.

That fear may have quickened his steps and set him running instead of conserving his energy. With the gun and the abundance of water in the Pine Barrens, he should have been able to keep himself alive a good long time, even in December and January.

But he was not used to that kind of situation, and he panicked and started to run, looking for an exit. Still, it was not a blind panic. The footsteps went in rushes and pauses as if he looked, decided, and then took off as fast as he could the way he had chosen. But eventually, the feet dropped to shuffle and not much further on they started to become erratic, where the heart attack probably happened.

I had followed his tracks around the heart-breaking

circles of the hopelessly lost. I had watched the circles get tighter and tighter as he speeded up, frantically looking for something that might lead him out. Not long after they began to shuffle, the tracks went erratic and began to stagger. He carried that heavy gun with him almost to the end.

I could see him in his tracks going along trying to use what skill he had but not sitting down and considering all the alternatives, not looking for solutions other than flight. Lost is probably when you can think of no other alternative to being where you are than flight. Maybe the pain kept him from hearing the traffic noises, and maybe he heard them after all and was trying to make for them through the blinding haze of his pain. He was going parallel with the Parkway when he finally fell, but he may have lost the direction of the sound. The place was far south on the untraveled part of the New Jersey Parkway, and there may well have been no traffic noises for him to follow.

All along his trail, I could see a resourceful man who, even in the first stages of panic, kept his wits about him and might well have made his way out of the woods, if his body had not given out on him, or it he hadn't pushed it so much. I could see him going to what he thought were the limits of his skills in the woods, and getting more and more afraid because those skills were leaving him just as lost as before.

Perhaps if he had said to himself that he would have to live off the land for a few weeks, he would have relaxed and come to the right trail eventually. Probably he did not think of all the organizational skills he used at other times in his life. I doubted that he organized his search for a way out as he would have organized a job. He had taken the gun, but he hadn't fired it to summon aid. Maybe he was saving that for the end when he couldn't go any farther. I looked at his trail for a long time and I wondered what I would do in a place as alien to me as the Pine Barrens had been to the hunter. I knew my skills were more than adequate to exist where I was,

but the hunter had skills that had allowed him to live the
day-to-day life of Northern New Jersey. He had had his
runs and his trails there, his snares to avoid and his survival drills to go through. I wondered how well my own
skills would work in other parts of the country. I went
off all the next four summers to find out.

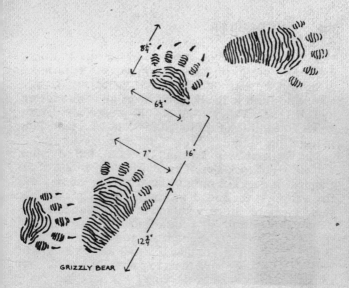

GRIZZLY BEAR

19/Bear Smacking

Over the next ten years I spent almost every summer testing my skills in different parts of the country; in the Dakota Badlands, Death Valley, the Grand Canyon, and the Grand Tetons. I first hitchhiked west when I was nineteen. I made California eventually, but I saw most of the other states either on the way there or on the way back. I slept in barns or in the woods in Pennsylvania, in the field in Ohio and Indiana.

I went to the Dakota Badlands to see if I could survive. I had ten dollars in my pocket when I left and after living off the land for three months and working my way as I went, I came back ten pounds heavier and ninety dollars richer.

Wherever I went, I tried to make contact with old trackers or hunters and with the Indians. I was very

lucky in that I was allowed to stay with a tribe I ran into
going up river in the Grand Canyon, and I learned a
great deal from the oldest man in the tribe. I learned
almost as much in the Badlands from an old wanderer,
and in Death Valley from an old prospector. Everywhere I went it seemed I found someone with something
to teach me.

The Badlands were arid and beautiful, full of gullies
and stands of rock almost as colorful as the rock of the
Painted Desert. The most difficult part of the stay was
the water. At the end, I was on my knees praying for
rain. I got rewarded with torrential downpours that
almost drowned me in a flash flood. Thereafter, I did
not seek divine intervention but worked, as Stalking
Wolf had taught me, to match myself to the patterns of
nature rather than bend them to suit me. I was hungry,
thirsty, or both most of the time I was out there, but it
did not exceed my limits, and as I adjusted to it, the
fascination of so much new to learn first-hand made me
enjoy my stay more, the longer I was there.

I watched the animals and tracked them. I watched
how their tracks deteriorated in the arid air, so I would
remember it if I ever had to track there some day. When
the summer was over, I had been hungry and thirsty and
still I had survived and had been content. I did not hear
an airplane for weeks at a time, and that alone almost
made it worth the trip. In the end, I was living well
enough not to want to leave.

Next, I tried Death Valley. It was a hotter anvil than
the Badlands, and the food was much scarcer. I left my
car with an Indian who owned a service station and told
him I was going to go live in the desert for six weeks and
that if I wasn't back out in nine, I was probably dead.
He snorted and said, "You ain't gonna live that long
anyways, so don't worry about it." I didn't bother
arguing with him.

I had a few cans of high protein food, and a knife,
and a piece of plastic to make a solar still. Stretched
down into a three foot hole with a rock in the center, the
sheet of plastic caught evaporating water on its un-

derside and funneled it down into the can in the bottom of the hole. I could get more than a pint a day in the driest place with my length of tubing stretched down into the can like a straw.

I lost track of time and spent almost eight weeks out there instead of six. I could have spent ten years there without scratching the surface of what there was to be learned.

I thought I had been thirsty in the Badlands, but Death Valley was a nightmare. The heat was worse as well, and I spent most days sleeping and then explored at night. I didn't expect to have much light to go by but I was surprised. After sunset, the landscape seems to turn an eerie blue. The stars are incredibly bright, and when the moon comes up, you can almost see to read a book. Everything else seemed to come out at night as well, and I was never without something to see or do.

The desert had a vastness to it that made me feel like the only spark of life in a dark, endless place. Time seemed to stretch away over the whole history of the desert, and I was in the middle of it, millions of years from its birth or death. I wandered without the restraints of place or time.

Things were easiest when I met some local Indians and was allowed to witness some of their ceremonies. Things were also easy the week I spent traveling with an old prospector who wandered the desert picking up enough gold nuggets a year to make him still believe that there was something worth finding out there. He was really well past any pleasure money could buy for him, and I believed the gold was only his excuse for living out where everybody else thought only a crazy man would live. I knew what he felt like. It seemed to comfort him that I would have lived his way gladly, but without the pretense of prospecting. He was a parched old man with a face like the weathering wood of a ghost town, and I learned a good deal just being around him.

The rest of the time, I lived alone, watching everything I could. I made camp in a large cave at the base of an outcropping of rock. I noticed that in the daytime I shared the cave with two rattlesnakes, and I was thinking of moving rather than having to kill them, but they seemed to sense that and seemed willing to ignore the ancient enmity between man and snake as long as I stayed on my side of the cave. The pack rats made no such compromises and stole my knife, which made the last few days an interesting test.

I ate lizards and snakes and a couple of other animals, but mostly it seemed, I ate sand and more sand. There was never anything to burn and a fire was rare, so a lot of what I ate went uncooked. Water was the big problem and thirst pushed me well beyond the limits I had had to pass in the Badlands.

But the desert was so full of life and beauty that I did not mind the thirst. A lot of times I went two or three days on half a canteen of water. When I ran out completely, I milked cactus. But at the end of the journey, I found again that I had not passed the ends of my resources. I had been hungrier and thirstier than I had been in the Badlands, but I had not reached my limits. I had learned a lot more about tracking and in the long run, it was worth far more than it cost.

The landscape in Death Valley defied description. But nothing was more indescribable than the Grand Canyon. I lived in it for a month, and it was never really credible to me that something that huge and that infinitely varied could exist. I could have learned all there was to know about tracking just following a trail from the subalpine rim of the canyon to the desert aridity of its floor. The canyon fascinated me, and I sat at every sunset and watched the impossible colors of the canyon wall change with the dying sun.

I swam in the Colorado River and went up and down its banks with my horse and pack mule. I learned every animal up and down that bank, I learned every rock and bush, and I loved every second of it. The canyon was like a time machine. Every foot I went down I went back into the history of the Earth, until I was millions of years away by the time I reached the canyon floor.

I worked all the levels, mining them for information.

I studied tracks at every level of the canyon and spent days going up and down the pack trail reading the variations as altitude changed the heat and humidity. I used to wait until just after the first mule train full of tourists had started back up and I would read the tracks and form descriptions of who had made them. Then I would catch up with the mules and check my descriptions. Each walk is so unique that I had no trouble matching the tracks with the people who made them.

I heard the howl of a coyote up the canyon one night, and the next day I went exploring up river, hoping to find a track or a skull. I found a tribe of Indians instead. There were two tribes actually although they had one name. One tribe lived up where the tourists could give them a living, and the other, made up mostly of old medicine men, camped in the ravine and kept the old ways. I went to the oldest and asked him to tell me his stories as I had done with Stalking Wolf. I sat there with him for two days listening as he told me the history of the canyon and its secrets. He was almost a hundred years old, but we had more in common than he had with some of the younger men.

I had grown up in similar ways, and we had an instant friendship. I believe he saw the hand of Stalking Wolf's teaching in me, and he accepted me instantly and taught me a great deal about tracking and about the unique way the spirit-that-moves-in-all-things moved through the canyon. We had a common heritage, and a common hatred for the men who had destroyed so much of the land. I wanted to stay with the Indians forever, but I had commitments and obligations. When the summer began to wind down, I moved west toward the final leg of my circle for that year.

I went to the Grand Tetons twice during my journeying, and for sheer beauty neither the Grand Canyon nor anyplace else, not even the Pine Barrens, topped it. I had seen the Rockies and the Sierra Madres, and I did not think I would ever see more impressive mountains; but when I first came in sight of the Grand Tetons, rising out of the plain, I was stunned.

There are some things that a camera trivializes, the Grand Canyon was one. It is too wide and too deep and too majestic to fit into the lens of a camera. The sheer scale of it cannot be reduced to inches and focal lengths. The Grand Tetons are the same. Other mountains are higher, but none are more beautiful. They seemed made of clouds, and in the middle of them the Snake River plunged over cliffs and sucked down around rocks on its way south, like a living thing.

I rented a pack horse and stayed in the mountains the whole summer. If there is a place nature lovers go when they die, it must look like the Grand Tetons. I wandered through them all summer long, poking in the abandoned villages and mining towns, climbing some peaks, floating down the Snake River in an inner tube past wide-eyed tourists going down the same rapids in huge rubber rafts. They shouted to me that I was crazy going down the most treacherous stretch of white water on the continent in an inner tube, but no one had bothered to tell me it was impossible before I did it. I shot past them, and when I looked back they were still shaking their heads at my craziness, as their raft caught the last rock and spilled them into the river.

Before long, I was out of the current and gliding along, slower than walking. The river was an open zoo. Moose ate at the side of the river as I floated by like a drifting log. Beaver paddled across my bow. Catfish nuzzled the inner tube. Trout jumped in the cool morning air. I floated without time or memory.

The tube went aground on its own, and went up the bank and along the river. I found the tracks of a moose before I had gone fifty yards. I had stumbled into one of his runs and I vowed to stay there until either he came back or winter did. I had to wait less than an hour by the side of the trail before he came past.

When he did, I could not believe how big he was up close! His head alone seemed to be a full-sized animal. I was so astounded at the size of his body that I stood up out of the bushes close enough to touch his flank as it went by. I could not see over him! Very quietly, I closed my mouth and crouched back down, hoping he hadn't noticed me. When he was gone, I got back in my tube and went on down the river, but it was not the same river, and I was not the same person I had been before I had seen the moose. I went away from it filled with awe and a sense of having been close to a completely new mystery.

But the moose was nothing compared with the grizzly. I saw my first one fishing at the side of the river as I went by on my inner tube, and the sight of him was greater than the sight of the mountains. For the first time, I realized just how difficult it would be to stalk up to a bear like that and smack it as Stalking Wolf's friend had tried to do. Bending over fishing, the bear was enormous. When he stood up, there was nothing in the forest half as tall, even the trees.

I knew he could run as fast as a horse, and for an instant, I wondered if he could swim as fast as the current was carrying me in my inner tube. But he had no interest in me, and I was staying as far outside his range as I could. Seeing him was the high point of an incredible day, but I was glad to get beyond even the illusion of being within his reach. I was still learning my craft, and I was no match for a grizzly and I knew it.

I had forgotten that particular limitation the next time I came to the Grand Tetons, and it almost cost me dearly. I still spent most of the year in the Pine Barrens between jobs, whose hours I whittled down until the job would disappear completely. I spent too much time in the company of people and too little in the woods for a while, and it was a bad point in my life when I went back to the Grand Tetons.

Even the trip out restored me, and I was full of the elation of having come alive after a long time of hibernation when I got there. I left my jeep at the ranger station and went out into the mountains. Everything was as wonderful as it had been before.

I lived more easily than the first time, and when I was ready to go home I knew I was going in the right direction again. It was probably that exuberance after such a

long staleness that made me overconfident. I saw the
bear on the way out as he was going over a little knoll
and into a glade. I stopped the jeep and got out.

I went up over the knoll following the smell of bear as
easily as its tracks. It was picking berries at the foot of
the knoll when I first saw it and I came up on it like a
moving shadow. I expected to smack it on the rump and
run away with a tale to tell Stalking Wolf when we met
again on the far side of the skull. I was about twenty
yards from it in a direct line, but there were two steep
rocks to climb down or make a thirty-yard detour. It
was probably that extra distance that saved me when the
twig broke.

It was carelessness that shamed me. I had gotten so
caught up in the majesty of the bear that I had moved
my foot without feeling where it was to come down. It
took the bear a second to locate me and I was already
running when he started to turn his head. I bounded out
of the trees and down a little hill to the jeep. I ran
beyond my abilities; if Rick had been there with a
twenty yard head start, I would have passed him by the
tenth step. But as I came down the hill, the bear was
right behind me.

I decided the jeep would be no protection and I
scrambled up the tree that ended in a broken split about
twenty-five feet high. The bear made a halfhearted effort at climbing and then stood up at full length and
swatted at me. I was as high in the tree as I could get and
sweating.

He was too heavy to climb, and I thought he would
get tired of leaning and looking up at the bottom of my
feet straddling the branch. But a grizzly bear is no wild
dog. He had no intention of waiting around, and he
stood on his hind legs again like a pick-up truck being
stood on its rear bumper.

When he slammed against the tree, the impact almost
threw me out of it. I could not believe someone hadn't
just run into it at high speed with my jeep. But one look
down into that angry face told me that I would have

been a lot better off if it had been a jeep. I had the feeling he was going to stretch up on his toes and slap me from the topmost branch. The second time he hit the tree, it picked up out of the ground and started to lean. For a minute I thought I saw him smile, and I got to a place where I could hang on in case the tree went down. But I had no time to prepare because he hit it a third time and pushed against it until it fell. I couldn't believe it.

Certainly the tree was old, but he had uprooted it just by leaning on it heavily. I was so amazed at the strength he had that I did not prepare my fall well enough. The tree landed with a crash, and it was only by dumb luck that I wasn't under it. The largest branch shattered into the ground, and the jolt of landing whipped me off the top and sent me tumbling toward the jeep. Only a lucky roll saved me, and I got to my hands and knees trying to clear my head.

I was stunned momentarily, but that would have been easily enough time for the bear if he hadn't been leaning on the bottom third of the tree with one paw, admiring his handiwork. He took two steps toward me and I was well under the jeep. I curled there, stuck on the horns of fascination and total terror.

The jeep shook as if something heavy had just run into it, and for a minute, I was afraid he was going to turn it over like a rock to get at me. But the jeep banged back down on its tires and I scrambled to the far side underneath. The size of the paw that reached under for me could not possibly have been as large as it seemed, but it tore off the muffler just the same and left it in shreds, slammed up against the rear tire. He did it with a mere flick of his wrist.

When I saw that impossibly big hand clawing under the jeep for me, I felt more naked terror than I had felt since the Jersey Devil had come to my camp when I was twelve. But legitimately frightened as I was, I was nowhere near panic. When the claw raked under the jeep I simply scrambled to the far side, almost out from under the jeep until he pulled that huge paw back out. I curled up and got as far away from those enormous claws as I could.

When he did not get me, he started on the jeep. There was a crash that picked up the front corner of the jeep and almost lifted it entirely off me. As it slammed back down, I could see the bumper flying end over end into the underbrush. The bang that followed it would have been enough to demolish the average car. But the Land Cruiser held solid. The jeep wallowed down over itself with the next blow and I knew that when I looked at my jeep again I would find the headlight and part of the fender missing.

He went around the jeep trying to fish me out with those huge claws from every angle. Every time he missed, he would pull his paw back with a roar of bad temper and slam the jeep. The headlights and tail lights were gone by the time he tried lifting the jeep again. He rocked it up off its wheels twice before he gave up on it and left me huddling near the far end. He moved around the jeep like a fox, going in one direction until I scrambled away from him, then reversing his field and taking a swipe under the opposite end of the car. At one point my face was inches from his hind foot while his front paw tore the air under the front part of the jeep looking for me. I found it so interesting that I forgot I was afraid and started to watch how the bear's foot curled up out of the ground leaving a perfect print. There were a million things I had questions about when I looked at the shaggy leg so close to my face. But he figured out where I was, and as he came lunging around, I scrambled backward and almost out from under the far side of the jeep. This time he stood up and I could not resist trying to see what he looked like standing that close. I slid forward and looked out at him under the radiator through a hole where the front bumper was supposed to attach. It was a mistake.

Just as I looked out, the bear roared out his rage and brought his paw slamming down on the hood like the fist of a drunken hunter making a point. I thought the jeep was going to break in two and leave me staring up at the bear without a hiding place. I felt like a mouse waiting for the cat to rip away its hiding place and devour it. I scrambled backward under the car and the bear reached over the hood. I heard the crash of the windshield going. The little squares of safety glass bounced like hail off the metal floorboards above my head. I waited for one more howl that would tell me he was about to pick up the jeep and break it in half. But eventually he got tired of pounding my jeep to get me out from under it. He came close a couple of times, when I was sure he was going to drive the frame down through the chassis and crush me. But I kept my head and moved in a tight little ball as far out of reach as I could get.

Finally, he stood up and up and up. He jerked the jeep to one side, lifted one wheel a foot, and let it fall. I heard the hood rip away like a boxtop and crash into the underbrush. I waited for the end, thanking the spirit-that-moves-in-all-things for the great opportunities to learn as much as I did and to see as much as I was fortunate enough to see. At last the bear got down on all fours and shambled away up the rise and into the trees again.

I was never happier to see a specimen go away, but I was also fascinated by what he had done. I crawled out a few minutes later and looked at the damage. It was spectacular. It was going to cost me long hours of boring work to get money to fix it, but it had been worth the price.

The smell of grizzly that close, the sound of his claws, like can openers, tearing up the metal, the swipe of his great hand that would have broken the neck of a bull as easily as it had snapped the lock bolts on my bumper and sent it spinning into the woods. It had been a small, continuing miracle. I went over the tracks for hours matching what he had done with the shape and placement of the print.

I stood by the jeep and recounted the damage as if I expected some of it to have healed. It would have to be repaired before I went much further west, and I would have to take a short job to pay for it. Still, it was driveable enough to get me out of there before the bear came back. Only his deep throaty growl from far in the woods set me reluctantly toward the trail again. All the time I was under the car, the world had been reduced to a horizontal plane of light between the bottom of the jeep and the ground where the bear's feet shuffled and danced in the dust. Everything of importance in the universe had happened within that narrow plane. Space had been reduced to a sliver, time to a moving point. The vividness of every detail still amazed and astounded me. Even as I leaned against the jeep, that impossible brightness still danced around me, and I rejoiced in the simple miracle of being alive.

I was there for a long time reconstructing it, but the bear never came back. I had overreached my limitations and lived to tell about it. Nothing was more exciting than that, and I swore to myself that I would not do it again. But it was not the last time I was inches from death.

About a week later, I was climbing a rock dome to get a better view, when I found myself past the safety mark of the curve and sliding toward the rim of the dome and the drop-off beyond it. I spread eagled and tried to dig my fingers into the stone, but I never got a decent handhold until I caught the raised lip of the rim as I slid over it. I hung there, too terrified to scream, trying to get one leg back up over the lip. I hooked a knee over the rim and hung there trying to gather enough strength in my rubbery arms to pull myself the rest of the way up while I caught my breath. I looked over both shoulders at the view: the sheer wall of rock patterned and etched for countless centuries, the spills of ancient stone sloping away from huge monoliths, the Snake River like a silver thread tying everything together.

If I had fallen then, I would have died happy with what I had seen. I expected at least the grand sights of my life to flash before my eyes when I felt myself going over the lip of the dome but instead I relived only one incident. For an instant, I was ten again, slipping down the curved dome off the water tower. I did not catch the rim that time and, until I hit the catwalk ten feet below, I experienced the perfect illusion of falling death. I was crazy to have climbed both places, but the best seats have always entailed the greatest risks, and I was always ready to pay the price. The bear had been a spectacular show.

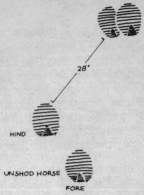

28°

HIND

UNSHOD HORSE

FORE

HIND

FORE

20/Outlaw Dogs

*In the pines, the wild dogs were their own justification.
They guarded the pines and ran free between the dumps
and the woods living off the land. They suffered the
outrages of winter, hunger, and cold; they had fat lazy
summers when the packs swelled with amateurs. They
moved within the pattern of the woods; they had a right
there and a duty. But by 1977, the packs had begun in-
creasingly to go bad.*

Politicians, pumping up business, and developers,
greedy for a short term profit, have been whittling away
at the Pine Barrens for years, and as more people came,
they came into conflict more often with the dogs. Over
the years, the Alpha pack had moved deeper into the
woods, but there were still isolated packs of dogs,

primarily wild from birth, who had left the woods and had begun killing livestock and attacking people.

I had been on dog hunts before, finding their hidden lairs for the police and the sharpshooters when a child had been mauled or a pet had been destroyed. I had dogs of my own, and the dogs of the pines had my grudging respect. I did not want to kill them, but there was no other choice.

The pack I had been asked to hunt had been killing sheep and harassing farmers for two years. Police had tried poison and traps, but nothing had worked, and they settled on the hunt as a last resort. The S.P.C.A. tried to make it harder by insisting on the use of tranquilizing darts, ignoring the fact that tranquilizers had to be administered in proportion to the body weight of the animal. If all doses were set for the weight of the biggest dog, half of the dogs would be killed by the overdose; anything less would leave the larger dogs unaffected. There was no way to stop a charging dog in the underbrush, guess his weight, calibrate the dart, and then shoot him with it.

The people who suggested it had never even seen a wild dog and knew nothing about them. They had the mistaken idea that the dogs were just cute little house pets with bad manners. They could not have been more wrong. The pack had developed a taste for blood and it was not going to go away. They had learned to kill for pleasure, like human beings.

I started out tracking around the farms that had been hardest hit. The southernmost of the three farms had not been bothered by the dogs for five or six weeks, but the northernmost had lost over $8,000 worth of sheep to the dogs. The farmer was angry and disheartened when he talked about it. He started to tell me what it had been like, coming out of his field in the morning, to find the mutilated sheep, some still not dead, lying around the field like the victims of a really bad car wreck. But he turned away and let the idea trail off into disgust and impotent rage. "They didn't even eat more than one or two of them," he said. "They just killed the rest for the fun of it.'' I had seen the police pictures of the mutilated sheep, and I knew what he must have felt like.

The farm in the middle had suffered the most. The woman there came out when she saw me looking at the tracks and offered any help she could give in catching the dogs. The pack had killed her cats and the family dog, and she hated them as much as her children did. After a few years, a dog or cat is like another child in the family, and their premature violent death is one of the worst traumas of childhood.

She told me how she had come out and tried to drive the dogs off after they had cornered her cat near the porch. But the dogs had ignored the broom and had turned on her and driven her into the house before they ripped the cat to shreds. I listened to her tell how she and the kids had carried the bloody body of the family poodle to the station wagon for the useless ride to the vet. She was almost beside herself when she started to talk about the dogs.

They had attacked her horse as well and pulled it down, tearing open its stomach and stripping the flesh off its back legs so that it lay all night in the field and had to be shot when her husband found it in the morning. After the horse, the dogs had gone after the people. ''They come running up on the porch howling and baying.'' she said. ''They just go round the house again and again all night long. The kids are afraid to go to sleep.'' The children had good reason to be afraid. The dogs had caught her son a little way from the house and had chased him home, snapping at his heels. The boy had dived through the storm door just ahead of the dog, who threw himself against the storm door and smashed its windows. The woman said she had fired three shots at it through the door, but had not hit it.

The dogs had chased her husband as well, treeing him for an hour until police came to drive them off. One of the dogs had even attacked a police officer, but he had killed it with his flashlight. The dogs had killed a calf there as well, just tearing it apart for sport as they had the horse.

"They never leave us alone," the woman said. Her voice was shaky with long strain. She asked me if I was going to kill the dogs, and I said I didn't know, I was just tracking them for the police and what would be done after that was up to them. She looked disappointed. "Well, if you kill them," she said, "I want the body of the big one." I cocked my head. "You want its body?!" She nodded. "I want to give it just one good kick," she said, "for what it did to Wintergreen." Her voice was helpless with anger and grief. I said I would do what I could. But I had no intention of dragging a body back for her, especially one as full of infection and disease as the wild dogs would be.

I had seen that kind of pack before, a litter of dogs abandoned in the woods and raised wild. They would be full of disease and infection, starved and emaciated, covered with wood ticks, bloated on bad blood and with ulcers left untreated. Some of them were almost certainly rabid, and the bite of any one of them probably carried a host of diseases.

The third farm had not been bothered for five or six weeks, but they had had their pets mauled. When the family shepherd had stood up to the pack, as it came marauding through, they had killed it. The other dogs and cats had all been bitten, and the family had been terrorized at night. None of them had any idea where the dogs came from or disappeared to.

There were not many tracks left around the third farm but there were worn runways connecting the first farm with the second and third. Runs coming out of the third farm came back toward the macadam road. All trails came to the same place, a hole in the fence of a government installation. I had no doubt they had gone in there, and I followed them in, wondering what I would tell the MP's if they caught me sneaking onto a government post.

The trail went in and skirted the C-shape garbage dump. It ran up into the trees and down into a steep natural amphitheater. They were laired up in a depression in the bottom of the bowl, a shallow recess covered with trees. I did not stay to watch them coming and going. When I reported where they were, the police got the permission of the base commander for us to go in and try to track them down.

There was no doubt in my mind that they were probably rabid, and killing them would be mercy. Rabies is a torment; the animal bites out of the unbearable frustration of his pain. I went in to the dump the next morning with three of my ex-Boy Scouts armed with shotguns. The police had allowed me to bring in my own people. I remembered the dog hunt I had tracked when I was sixteen, a bloodbath of indiscriminate shooting. It had been a wonder that no one had been killed, except one pet dog and most of the pack. I did not want to see that happen again nor did I want to find myself driving the dogs out of hiding again and into a hail of shotgun fire that is also coming at me.

Harsh necessities drove me. The dogs were my responsibility. They had their corrective duties in the woods, and I had mine. I went to the dump and climbed a slope into the woods on the far side of it. The big Alpha dog saw me and dove back into the woods. I watched the dogs a while and then went back to the jeep and put out the bait. The dogs charged over the lip of the hill a little later, and came at a full run down the slope. We opened fire before they were fully down. Two turned to run, the rest charged. I saw one of my boys fire three times at a charging dog and hit him all three times without knocking him off his feet. In the end, he had to club it aside with the stock of his gun, as the dogs overran us. The gunfire turned some of them around, and four of the nine remaining dogs ran back up into the woods. The police killed four more of those who had run past us, but we were faced with going into the underbrush after the others, where the advantage would be all theirs. When we got out of the woods, we found there were even greater obstacles.

According to a reporter, the S.P.C.A. was supposed to be suing me for having killed the dogs. First I was hurt, and then I was angry. I could not understand people like that. They acted as if I was a sadist out killing dogs for fun. It was hard, dirty work, and I did not like doing it. But I believed it had to be done. The dogs could not be left to roam free, killing at will.

The SPCA's suggested alternatives were ridiculous at best. The dogs could not be trapped or poisoned. It was not even certain that they could even be hunted successfully. We could not get close enough to them the whole morning to get a shot, and they had circled around us most of the afternoon. The SPCA wanted them driven into nets.

According to the rumor, the lawyer was going to sue me for organizing the hunt even though I had written authorization from the chief of police and he was going to have me prosecuted for not holding the dogs five days before killing them. It seemed completely crazy to me. But most of what I saw outside the woods seemed insane, and I believed it was true.

I had an absolute horror of courtrooms. They seemed to me the most intricate and frightening of all institutions. They were so complex that even citified people did not enter one without a lawyer to explain what was going on. Even the thought of hiring a lawyer seemed terrifying. Lawyers had to be so *crafty* to do what they did, that even if they were on your side, it would be like being friends with a fox. What was worse, when it came to lawyers, I couldn't tell a fox from a wolf, or a wolf from a wild dog. When I heard the rumor, I wanted to pack up everything and leave.

But it was not as simple as that. If I let myself be scared off from what I knew was right, I would have to accept the responsibility for what would happen. If I stopped hunting until everything went through the courts, the dogs would be long gone, and not until they had struck again would I be able to find their trail again. Even if it only took a week, a thunderstorm during that time would have wiped out everything. It had taken three days to pick up and follow their trail, the next time might take a lot longer. I would have to take responsibility for all the damage those dogs would do until I tracked them down again if I let them get away.

Sooner or later, the dogs would catch something small and human out in the open. Only a week before, a domestic dog had torn a baby out of its carriage and would not stop gnawing on its head even when two men beat and kicked it. The child survived, but I would not want the memory its mother carries. I had been too close to those teeth too often not to have sympathy for the victims. A wild dog would have gone for the throat. I would not be responsible for letting that happen.

The worst of the dogs were still out there. Both the Alpha and the Beta dog had gotten away. Alpha was the leader only by virtue of his size, and the meaner Beta dog challenged him constantly. It may well have been the rivalry between the two lead dogs that turned the pack to killing for the sake of killing. Howling around the house at night and attacking people in their front yards may have been outbreaks of the power struggle within the pack, as each of the leaders tried to outdo the other in daring and viciousness. It was a battle that would go on as long as both of them were alive.

If I waited until morning, they would be gone. They would have gone back to the lair after the attack to form the survivors into a pack again, and when it got dark, they would move somewhere else. Even if the judge laughed the SPCA out of court in the morning, the pack would be gone. There was nothing to do but go back out. I took my 8mm Mauser and a slip of shells and crawled down a hundred yards of dog run to the top of the amphitheater. The moon was rising as I crawled, and when it was full up they would come pouring over the lip of the depression and down the runs.

I crawled forward until I could hear their growls, then I slipped off the run and into a clump of brush to wait for the moon to rise. I listened to the night, insect sound, animal sound, wind sound. Everything seemed to blend together, the thatch of pine needles pressing against my jeans was one with the musty, downwind odor of the dogs.

I had rubbed skunk cabbage leaves over my body to kill my scent, and I had come up the wind. If I was going to get all of them, it was necessary for them not to know I was there until it was too late. Any dogs I missed would be gone, free to ambush me on my way back out and I had no doubts that that was what they would do. The pack had the same military precision I had seen in the Alpha pack, and an ambush was a maneuver I had seen wild dogs pull a number of times. In the dark, with surprise on their side, the odds were in their favor. I came alert to the sound of claws scrambling over the rock lip of the lair as the dogs ran toward me in the night.

I took them as they came up the slope toward me. All I could see of them was their eyes and the vague dark shadows of their bodies. They came toward me silent as ghosts. They might just as well have been the spirits of the dogs leaving. I stood and killed them as they came.

The Alpha dog died hard. The fifth bullet dropped him near my feet, but he wriggled close enough, while I fired again, to sink his teeth into my boot. I kicked him away and fired at the next animal up the slope. He was dead by then anyway. When I had the chance to think again, I wondered how much pain it took to generate that kind of rage. I had had no time to count the dogs. They had come in bunches after the Alpha dog's charge. The only rational thought I remember having was that I might not have enough ammunition, and then everything was still. The silence seemed to roar with echoes. I almost didn't hear the claws going up the far bank.

The Beta dog had gone down in a tumble in the first wave out of the lair; the bodies of the other dogs littered the slope. Running last up the hill, he must have seen that, and decided there was no pack left but himself. Of all the dogs, he was the one I would never have let escape. I would have gone into that dark after him with a knife if I had to.

The Alpha dog had proved himself the leader in the end, charging up the slope at the head of the pack, but the Beta dog was something far more dangerous, a natural survivor. I admired him for that, but he was far too deadly to be let escape to start another blood pack somewhere else. I killed him with the first shot, short and clean.

I stood looking down the dim slope at the bodies for a moment, wishing I did not have to go down among them. But I went, hoping they were all dead, and shot those that still seemed to be alive. I tried not to look at them. They were starving, sick, and diseased dogs, scrambling against impossible odds to stay alive. They were full of sores, all cracked and broken open. Ticks the size of my thumb clung to them all over. Their ears were masses of chiggers and unhealed wounds. The Alpha dog had a deep abscess in his side that must have driven him crazy when he ran fast.

It was hard to say why they had become outlaws: from the craziness of pain, from the frustration of un-ceasing hunger, for pleasure, or to prove a dominance. It did not matter. I had had no thought of vengeance, and I had no thought of remorse. It was a hard job, and I had done it, but I did not like it and I did not want to do it again. I hauled the bodies down into the swamp. The swamp sucked them under and buried them. Even-tually only their bones would hang suspended in the mud, waiting for the spade of some fossil hunter's curiosity to free them. I dug out a pit and watched them go under and down into the soft mud. It was probably softer than any place they had lain down during their lives.

In the morning I would get my summons, I supposed, but I had done what I thought was right. If there were punishments for that, I was ready to take them. When the last dog was in the ground, I picked up my gun and trudged back up the rise.

It had been a hard track, and even harder stalking. I had used much of my knowledge and most of my skill, and I was proud of the way they had worked. But there was no elation in it. I had done a difficult thing well, but I could not exult.

It did not seem the true thing for which I had trained so long, and I wondered where in the scheme of things I was supposed to be. As I looked down the slope, I knew that it was not there or anywhere like it. It was false dawn when I got back to the jeep, and the birds were just coming awake, but true dawn was just behind it, and the sun rose as I drove away like the promise of something better.

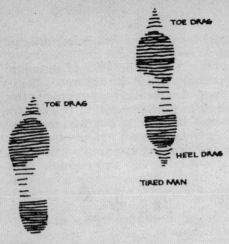

TOE DRAG

TOE DRAG

HEEL DRAG

TIRED MAN

MODERATELY TIRED MAN

21/Search

Tracking is grueling work. I go over the ground faster than a dog locked on a scent, and I have collapsed during a search more than once because my fascination with the trail drove me without stopping. The trail stretches out in front of me like something about to dissolve, and I go tracking down it like someone possessed.

When I get that trail, I follow it with all my concentration. Everything else disappears, except the trail and the person at the end of it. Usually, time is crucial. I rarely get into a case before hundreds or thousands of searchers have churned up the ground looking without success, and it takes the longest part of my time to find the first print in the chain.

But when I do, it's like a reflex from then on, and I go

charging down the trail, picking out each print, filling in the ones that are missing, watching the personality emerge from the tracks, reading the flow of energy in the depth of the footprint. Sometimes the track is hard to come by, and sometimes there is only tragedy at the end of it. But most of the time, especially if I can get to the track early, there is a lost hunter, or a family, or a child at the end of the trail.

There is nothing in the world that can compare with the sense of joy, accomplishment and rightness that comes with finding a person still alive that everyone else has given up for dead. Every time it happens to me, I have the same intensity of feeling that I had the first time, but there is one time that stands out above all others, because at the end of that trail I found myself.

It happened in 1977. It seemed to me that for ten years I had been asked over and over why I wasn't in college, why I didn't have a permanent 9-to-5 job, why I wasted so much of my time running around in the Pine Barrens, and I had begun to wonder if perhaps my life really *was* a waste after all. I had begun to wonder if I hadn't just mistaken a fascinating hobby for a lifetime purpose. As some people I knew were fond of pointing out, I not only wasn't rich and famous, I hadn't even achieved the commonplace. I had no job, no house, no family, no life insurance, and no sit-on lawn mower. I began to wonder what my purpose in being alive was, and where I fit in the scheme of things. The trail of a person I will call Tommy changed all that.

Tommy was a five-year-old boy in a man's body. He had aged thirty-one years, but he had the same shy innocence he had had at five. He loved picnics. He loved to go into the woods with his father, who was getting too old to go into the woods with ease. One Saturday, he packed a lunch, put on two pairs of pants and two sweaters; he carried another sweater along with him. He wore one pair of boots and carried another. He also took along several of his favorite record albums to listen to in case he got lonely.

By late Saturday, a S.W.A.T. team, a helicopter, two dog packs, and a thousand soldiers, police, and volunteers were in the area searching. Papers carried stories of the retarded man lost in the woods and speculated on his chances as the temperature fell or it began to rain. It was early May, but the weather was still late March, and twice it dropped to freezing. One day it rained. By the fourth day, they had unofficially given up.

It was improbable, they said privately, that a five-year-old could be outside in that kind of weather for four nights and still be alive. I think the police had thought of Tommy as a five-year-old so often that they forgot that his body was considerably older and stronger than his logic. I found out about the search Wednesday morning and called the police to offer my services. The chief told me to report to a captain who looked at me as if I told him I was a witch when I told him I was a tracker.

"So you're the great tracker who's gonna find this kid and make us all look like fools," he said. He had the most sarcastic smile of any man I had ever met. "Well, you can go look, but you're not going to find anything: there's been a thousand men through here, and it's going to rain pretty soon, good and hard."

"Why don't you just show me where you lost the trail," I said.

He looked sheepish. "We'll show you where we think he went." He showed me a map with the house on it. The bottom land and gravel pit southwest of it had been thoroughly searched. I said I would need to see a pair of his shoes and to talk with his parents first, and the captain assigned me a patrolman either by way of punishment or because he looked least busy.

The father wavered between hope and despair. He said Tommy was especially shy of strangers and was probably running from the searchers, if he was still alive. I said I'd look and asked the sergeant to show me Tommy's tracks. It turned out that they had never found any tracks. They took me to a dirt road they thought he had gone down for no other reason than that

that was the way they would have gone. It was not where I would have gone.

It began to rain and the patrolman said he would wait in the car. I nodded, and when he was gone I walked back up to the house and started criss-crossing the back of the property, looking for his tracks. On my second pass I found them. The incongruity of the mansized footprints and the almost skipping walk made an unmistakable gait. The tracks went at a 90-degree angle to the road, and the vast area of bottom land that had been trampled through by searchers. The trail led into some thick woods behind the house where Tommy had been used to going on picnics with his father before his father had gotten so strangely small and slow.

It was a hard track from beginning to end. The trees were thick and the brush between them was even worse. Thorn vines twined through interlocking shrubs and wild hedges, making the whole groundcover a waist-high mat. If I could have found a deer trail and gone on all fours in a low crouch, I might have gone quickly and easily through the woods. But I had to follow the tracks, and the tracks were harder than any I had ever seen to put together into a trail.

I needed a logic to thread them together. The logic of a fox, a rabbit, an otter is easy to comprehend. Curiosity, whimsy, and passion for variety do not seem to count for much with them, and it is easy to look ahead down the unseen part of the track toward where you know there will be water or food and a good place for that kind of animal to live or lay over while traveling.

A fleeing man is even easier; his way through the woods will vary with his personality, but either he will go *through* whatever is in his way, or he will pick the easiest route around it. In either case, his logic is escape, and the quickest way will always take precedence over the easiest.

But Tommy's logic was a bewildering blend of sharp pragmatism and erroneous assumption. He sometimes started out to do a thing without any idea of how to go about it, and his tracks were often a bewildering maze until I realized that for most of the trail, his tracks were like mine. Every few feet, they went off on a tangent after something interesting.

He was a mixture of reason and whim that was hard to make sense of, and I spent as much time figuring out a track once I found it as I had taken to find it in the first place. I had one piece of luck: the ground was soft and wet but firm enough to make an excellent track and hold it a good long time despite the drizzle. A downpour would wash the tracks away or soak them into oblivion, but even four days had not made them invisible. It was four o'clock when I started to track, and it was getting dark when I finally came out of the woods.

The rain was coming down harder, and I was soaked. The soft ground I had come through was lower than the stream and the ground was dissolving with water, unwrinkling the prints. By morning, there would be nothing to follow if I did not get a trail and follow it to high ground and a solid track. Without that one good track, it might take days to find the parts of his trail that were still trackable.

On the far side of the woods, there was a chicken coop and when I looked in it, I found lay marks in the old straw. There were prints under the doorway where he had crawled up and in. His toes were dragging, and they had been dragging for the last hundred yards. The plumes of dirt in front of each print had softened to puffs of smoke, but the faint unshaped toe and the rim of the hard-hit heel said he had come to the abandoned chicken coop at about four on Saturday afternoon and had slept in the coop for a few hours.

He was a small man and heavyset. He toed out in an irregular way, and he was not in good condition. His walk was not strong, but it had the endurance of fascination, and when he matched both goal and route, he could move at a good pace for a surprisingly long way. He was dropping things every so often on his way to the coop, but he did not leave anything in it.

I crawled back out of the coop and went over the

tracks looking for later prints, and I found them easily. They went south from the chicken coop. I was losing the light and I was getting worried. The ground sloped gradually away from the coop down into a softer almost marshy area with a stream running through it. If the rain kept up, the ground would be too wet there to hold a track, and I would have to begin circling on the next piece of solid ground, a process that might take me a day and a half.

If I had one print on solid ground that the drizzle wouldn't affect, I would be all right. But the light was going more and more rapidly as I pressed on toward the stream. The worse the light got, the closer I had to get to the ground. I moved on all fours a lot in the woods. It is simply the fastest way to move. The animals like the deer who make the runs, wear away tunnels in the growth that don't grab at every step. Using the runs in dense growth saves a lot of energy, but you have to go in a crouch and all fours is the easiest way. After a while it becomes habitual.

I scramble along a trail like a half mad toad leaping from one track to the next. I go like a dog, running along the ground or stopping motionless trying to catch what shade of disturbance has caught the eye of my training. If I look long enough I always find it.

I went flying over the ground at first, but I went slower and slower as the light went, until I came to the stream bank. I would have seen his treasures easier in the daylight, but I had no doubt that that was where he had sat to rest.

I looked at the broken fiddleheads. He loved the small curved plants, and I had found them broken off all through the woods. Wherever a print took a funny angle I could be sure he had bent while going by and plucked one off with a sweep of his hand. I loved the way he traveled, scooping everything up on the fly like that.

The prints had staggered going away from the chicken coop, and I could see him waking up out of a terrible dream about going on a picnic and getting lost. The hay was thrashed where he woke up startled and bewildered, and there was a touch of helplessness in the way the track wove right and left as if stopping every few feet to beg aid from someone who wasn't there.

I could see him holding his hands cupped in one another and talking to himself, telling himself not to be afraid, that his daddy would come, trying to figure out where he was. His feet dragged for a while as the sense of lostness overwhelmed him. But he did not let it panic him. If he sat down and cried about his predicament, he did the least of what people who are lost do when they think they are gone forever. He had not panicked. I prayed that he was still alive, because I loved anybody who could go from the dragging feet of despair to skipping less than fifty feet later.

Once he had decided that he was lost, he set out to explore until his father came for him. He ran a little, but he tired easily, and he must have taken a long time going in, meandering through the low land. The prints were getting fainter, but they were at least regular for a while.

I got closer and closer to the ground as the light went, until I was feeling the prints as Rick and I had done when we tracked the Rabbit King in the grass. But the rain was soaking them and tugging them back into a smooth, loose line. The trail wavered a little as he followed something I could not see to track, and if he had gone on in that way, I would have lost the trail to the rain. But just when I thought it was going to dissolve in front of me there in the damp lowland woods, the trail suddenly started moving straight and active toward higher and more solid ground.

I had been on my hands and knees in the soggy ground a dozen times trying to find the next straight step in his winding erratic course. But once he started for the rise to the south, he went straight for it with a singleness of purpose most people could not have generated.

I went scrambling after him covered with mud, scratched by thorns, cold, and tired. I had been running on all fours, crouching, climbing, walking, jumping, crawling, doing most of the things he had done in a full day, in only four hours. I had a good idea where his footprints would be up on top of the rise when I got there but following them out of the swamp would save me precious time in the morning.

It was full dark when I followed the last footprints up the rise, feeling them with the tips of my fingers brushing back and forth as Stalking Wolf had taught me. I reached out the length of his stride and moved my hand over the width of his straddle. I felt for the diagonal line of his foot as it toed outward or for the last fading wedge of a heel print. He was hitting hard on the toes because of the incline, and the prints were ever deeper than I needed to get along them quickly.

I was tired, and I wanted to stop, but I had to have a solid print the rain would not take completely away. Finally I collapsed, panting, on top of a good one a little way off the dirt road. The police assumed he was running away, although they never said why, and they assumed that he would logically take the nearest road. But he had come to the road by a circuitous route and to a large extent by accident.

The road was familiar to him, but there is not nearly as much of interest on a road as there is off in the woods alongside it, and that was where he had walked. I understood that. It was where I would have walked, and I could see the fascination with small and ordinary things that characterized my own walk. I might as well have been tracking myself the way it wound and meandered.

I had no doubt that the trail that I would pick up in the morning would begin wandering no more than fifty yards down the road. Still, I had a solid track. It was three days old, but I knew it would lead me to him, if he survived the night. I believed he was still alive, and I knew the odds were a lot more in his favor than the police thought they were. He had taken shelter again. He had eaten a couple of his sandwiches as he walked, and hunger was a problem more than a threat.

If he kept sucking on the fiddleheads he plucked, eventually he would get hungry enough to eat them, and they alone would keep him going for a while. He was capable of finding his own shelter and with a little luck I believed he would make it. His track showed a gift for seeing the wondrous that I almost envied. He may have been worried that he was lost, but it did not dampen the delight he seemed to find every few feet.

I hoped he would find himself shelter from the storm and something to eat. I went out and made a marker in the road opposite the track and backtracked to where I had found his lunch and clothes. He had left the albums stacked, as if he had expected to come back for them once he got himself oriented. They were not just dropped, and except for that heartbreaking shuffle of helpless tracks just outside the chicken coop, he had not given way to panic or despair. I did not know many people with Ph.D.'s who could have kept themselves alive as well.

I lay on the track, deciding whether to go on all night. If I tracked by feel all night, I might move a quarter of a mile up his trail by morning. In daylight, it would be an hour's work. The tracks I was following were still from Sunday, and I knew that unless he was dead, I was not within easy reach of him in the dark. So, I picked myself up and went back and collected his valuables and took them to his father for identification.

The father said they were Tommy's, and he looked at me as if he expected me to say I had found them near a body. But his eyes said that the true feelings of a parent did not tell him Tommy was dead, and that until he felt it in his heart, he would not give up believing in Tommy's safe return. I told him I could not be sure, but that I believed Tommy was still alive, that he had been taking cover and foraging for food and had a chance of surviving. I had his trail and by the end of the next day I would know how close I was.

I took the clothes and records with me to the car; the sergeant threw his cigarette out the window and took me down to the firehouse to report. I was still wet and muddy, and my arms were scratched. I looked like I had been dragged up and down the road behind a car. The sergeant looked at me like I was enjoying getting mud on the seatcovers. I was too tired for either an argument or an apology and I said nothing. He drove off.

Only forty men were left after sunset, and most of those had gone home or back to the firehouse for a quick beer after a hard day. They had spent a long day in the woods and they had come up with nothing. The woods were too thick for even the dogs to pick up a scent. They were all sure he was dead. If they were troubled by it, it didn't show. The fire chief looked me up and down and shook his head like a mother who is going to have to wash the clothes. "Did you have fun playing in the rain, Piney?"

I had the jacket bundled up under my arm. They saw nothing but the mud anyway. I said nothing. The chief looked like he would have washed me out of any training program he'd ever run. "Well, tracker, what did you find?"

I unfolded the jacket and took out the lunch bag and slammed it on the table in front of him. "There's his lunch! There's his extra shirt! There's his hat! There's the record albums he took with him, and there's his extra shoes." I spread the jacket over all of them. "And here's his coat. He's alive. He's been living in chicken coops and things and eating his lunch and fiddleheads."

There was a stunned and awkward silence that deepened with each object I slammed down on the table. The silence hung in the air for what seemed like an hour. The fire chief shook his head in rueful disbelief like a man who has bluffed against a full house. Then he turned over his shoulder and shouted, "Hey, Larry, get the tracker a beer." I took a coke by way of compromise because I did not want to reject his hospitality. If I had thought about it, I suppose in their position I would have been sceptical too. Besides, I was used to it. I told them what I had found where and they were full of questions about how I had done it.

When I left, the chief asked if there was anything I

needed, and when I said I didn't think so, he said they would give me a walkie-talkie I could direct the helicopter with when we got close. If he still believed I wouldn't get that close, it didn't show in his face.

The next morning it was drizzling, but the rain cleared off by midday. The second day was more grueling than the first. The temperature was way below normal, and the drizzle had a late winter sting to it. I was wet before I started, but the trail looked promising, and I was anxious to get at it.

Tommy had been holding his own, but he had been lucky, and I was worried. So many days had passed between when he had started and when I had. The trail ran parallel with the road for a while and I went flying along it, watching the zig-zags come back into it. I think he was going the wrong way and didn't realize that the landmarks he recognized every once in a while should have been running in the other direction. Maybe he was just happy to see something familiar.

Once he seemed to himself to be on the road for home again, his curiosity took over and his trail went in butterfly loops and flitters along the road and then down toward the stream. The ground softened up a little, but the prints still held. And then they disappeared.

I had to go slowly and track by the broken branches and kicked-over stones. Even where the prints were good, the briars had thickened up and the undergrowth was almost inpenetrable. I was scratched bloody before I had gone half an hour. The trail went up one rise after another, and the tracks got fainter as they went uphill. I had to track along the ridge by misplaced stones and broken branches over hard terrain.

After the second rise, I skipped going up any hill or ridge and went around them looking for the tracks coming back down again. They were always clearer in the softer soil of the bottom of the slope, and it saved me hours. Sometimes he would come down a little left of where I expected, but generally he came down the right side as a right-hander would.

He crossed the stream, but the trail was easy to pick up on the other side of it. The ground went uphill again, and the underbrush got thicker and thicker. I had been going for several miles through very rough territory as fast as I could, and I was out of breath. I was sweating with the exertion, but my hands were cold and my fingers were frozen from running through the wet grass or grasping the wet branches to see how they were broken and when.

I found two more lay spots where he had stopped to rest, and I believed that he must have come out on the macadam road very late in the day. But his tracks ended at the road. They had a number of soldiers waiting along the road to be told where to go in, but there was nothing I could tell them. The tracks had come out onto the hardtop late Saturday, and there was only one way to find where he had gone from there. A half hour later, I was walking a twenty foot zigzag across the road, from one shoulder to the other, looking for the tracks he would have begun to make when he came off the road again.

I found them about two hundred yards north on the left side of the road. From the road, they went to the farmhouse, but there must not have been anybody home, and probably the dogs frightened him away. Near the lay spots near the stream, I had found places where he had knelt and hid, probably from the searchers. It must have been terrifying for him, all those strangers calling his name, all that noise, those dogs barking, and that helicopter going back and forth over his head like it was after him.

I could see his pace pick up. They must have been in the woods after him after his nap, and he heard them and took off. Well behind the farmhouse there was an old chicken coop and a good warm barn. I followed the tracks to the chicken coop and looked inside. I found his lay marks in the straw where he had slept. From there, his prints went across to the horse barn. But between the two, the prints went back and forth in a bewildering pattern of running, crouching, scurrying, back and forth like a mouse going between food and its hole.

He must have slept in the horse barn and then moved to the abandoned chicken coop before anyone got up. He had been raised on a farm, and he knew the hours. There was a lot of fear and indecision in some of the tracks, as if sometimes he went back to the coop out of boredom or to get something, and at other times, he was trying to hide.

Either the people had been away, or he had kept out of sight remarkably well. There was a hint of play in the footsteps as well, as if he was certain he was hiding for his life from the strange men but couldn't divorce it from the game of hide and seek. When I went over to the horse barn, I knew he was still alive somewhere.

In the horse feed, which comes as a sticky mixture of grain and molasses, someone had ignored the scoop and clawed out a handful to eat. I went around the room and found more of it dropped in the corner of one of the stalls, where he had apparently cowered and gobbled it down. There were some old apples lying in a half barrel, and he had gotten into them and eaten the cores and what was still edible on them. He had nibbled the corn that had been left lying around as well. He had kept himself better fed than I had been able to do in Death Valley, and every time I found something of his, my admiration for him grew. He had, according to the tracks, stayed there probably Sunday, Monday, and Tuesday, which meant he had been in the relative warmth of the horse barn when the temperatures had dropped below freezing and the searchers started looking for the blue fringed corpse that the freeze should have left them.

It took me a long time to decipher the tracks, to figure out how long he had been there and when he had left. Apparently, he had gone away from the barn on Wednesday in the morning when the weather had been better and had gone exploring north. A mile or so down the road, I followed his tracks around the perimeter of a large dog pen. He had come close to it and then jumped back and started running away from it, probably as the dogs had come howling and barking toward the fence.

The dogs came barking toward me as well as I went past, and the woman who owned them came out to see what was going on. She said the dogs had been disturbed Wednesday morning and again later in the day. I knew we were getting close to him.

His trail crossed the stream again and went through more rough country. But I was getting more and more worried. Unless we found him before nightfall, he was probably going to have to spend the night in the open, and I was not sure how much strength he had left. There was still an exuberance in his walk, but it slid into the shuffle of fatigue more and more often as the struggle wore him down.

By the time I recrossed the road, I had spent another three hours of steady moving on the trail. When I find a trail, I move along it with total concentration, and I sometimes run into things. Stray branches had caught me in the head or tore at my arms, and I had deep scratches almost everywhere that kept bleeding. But there was no time to stop and clean them up, just so they would look good. My total absorption in the track kept the pain away. Nothing kept away the frustration.

I stopped at the side of the road gasping, in almost complete despair. I had been so close to him so often, I could almost see his feet leaving the marks I was beginning to pick up. But the going had been alternating runs and dead stops, all of it through the tightest tangle of brush and vines that I had ever tracked through before. I had gone over equally bad country following deer, but then I could go down the same path of least resistance the deer had worn down.

But this was practically a continual fight through almost jungle-thick undergrowth. I had been at it for seven hours, and I was exhausted. My breath came in gasps and my hands stung with numbness. I looked at the road and cursed. I had come so far, and I knew I was close, so close!

I almost cried I wanted to find him so badly, but my

body did not want to go any further. I sat slumped at the side of the road. If his track was not straight across, it would take hours to find it. I would have to snake back and forth across the road again, and the warming trail I could feel bringing me nearer to him would go cold.

I had come to the breaking point again. I was tired and thirsty and frustrated beyond words because it was taking me so long to find him when neither of us had the time. The temperature was going to go down below freezing again, and I did not think he could find his way back to the horse barn as he had when the dogs had frightened him. If we didn't find him soon, I was not sure he would make it.

I sat looking forlornly at the road. Out at the edge of your will and stamina, there is always a place where you come upon despair. Maybe it's a thing of the blood. The waste products build up with extended exertion and your spirit plummets like the twenty-mile depression of the marathoners. I had had it before and I waited for it to burn past me and leave me in the flowing center of energy that always followed the crash.

In a few minutes I was asking myself what the hell I was sitting there for like I had nothing better to do than feel sorry for myself. I got up and crossed the road, and there on the other side, almost directly in line, was the rest of his trail. I looked at it with elation. The prints were almost new, I was almost tripping his heels.

I felt the rush of my second wind go through me, and I plunged into the underbrush with a little cry of joy. I knew he was only a little way ahead of me, and I could feel myself getting stronger and stronger. But the woods were the worst of all I had been through, and instead of a mat of branches tied together by the creeping thorny vine, there were whole patches of briars to be gone around.

But Tommy had not gone around them; he had ducked down to deer-high and had gone low, crawling on his hands and knees down the runs. I went after him in the same way, but I was a lot bigger, and the briars tore at me until my shirt was in tatters and there did not seem to be a running inch on my arms or face that was not scratched. I was a smear of blood and mud, but I kept pressing after him.

I would have overtaken the brightest Ph.D. in a few hours, but Tommy stayed outside my grasp, tormenting me, and I wondered what all that training was for, and all that suffering and learning when I couldn't get the man who was running just beyond my reach, perhaps to his doom. I was almost about to let the helicopter boys have it when I found the first of his footprints in the swamp. They were just beginning to fill with water!

I stifled a shout of joy. He was within hearing distance. I was right behind him. I crashed across the swamp and picked up the trail again. I groaned when I saw where it went.

The briar patch must have been fifty yards across, and he had gone down on his knees into it. If I went around, I would lose precious time. If I went through, I was going to have to pay a heavy price I didn't think I could pay. I knew he could be no further away than the far side of the briars and I called the helicopter to come in about a hundred yards ahead of me. A second or two later, it clattered in over the land on the far side of the briars.

I heard the pilot shouting that he saw him lying down but apparently alive. I gave a sigh of relief. The helicopter pilot gave his report and someone ordered the troops along the roadway to come in through the woods to surround him. They closed in on three sides, leaving only the briars in front between us. He was alive and that was all I cared about.

I slumped down and let the tiredness that I had been holding back so long wash over me. All I wanted was a hot bath, hot coffee, and a long sleep. My walkie-talkie crackled as the helicopter swayed back and forth over Tommy, trying to shout down to him with the bullhorn. I paid no attention to it until the pilot shouted, "He's running! Oh, hell, he's running again!" There was only one place he could run and that was into the briars, but

if he made it back in at any other place than the run I
was in front of, we might never find him.

The soldiers were still too far away from him to stop
him. I plunged into the briars. The runs beneath them
were far too small most of the time, and the dayglo vest
they had given me was nothing but strips of cloth by the
time I came out the other side. My flannel shirt was
shredded and my thermal undershirt was ripped from
neck to waist and flapped open as I ran. I can't think of
a place I did not have a thornscrape or a tear.

I came staggering out of the briars in time to see the
S.W.A.T. team running at him from the other side of
the clearing. He had stopped running not 20 yards from
where I was and I ran toward him. He had fallen to the
ground and was cringing there. The helicopter clattered
above him shouting instructions that disintegrated ten
feet below the bullhorn. Tommy seemed to be waiting
helplessly for the strange men to do whatever terrible
things strange men did when they caught someone. The
S.W.A.T. men got to him first. They were happy to
have found him, but they were more afraid that he
would run away again, and they wanted a good hold on
him more than anything else. They pulled him to his
feet, and he struggled. But they were very big men and
he had no chance. Still, he kept thrashing and I admired
his courage as much as I had admired his resourcefulness. He made sounds that were too terrified to be
speech and the soldiers tightened their grip on his arms
to keep him from getting away again.

He looked like the rabbit who is about to turn and
lash out with everything he has because the only other
alternative is death. His scream pried his mouth open,
and I peeled the wrapper off the Tastycake I had been
carrying tucked in the pocket of the vest. I stuffed it into
his mouth and his fear melted.

He stopped resisting and the soldiers loosened their
grip. Tommy pulled free and threw his arms around me
and hugged me as if he had been waiting for me to come
and get him for a long time. I put my arms around him,
and he began to cry the way only a child can when he's

safe enough to afford the luxury. He had come a long way on his own. He had survived when nobody believed he could. He had overcome obstacles everyone thought utterly beyond him.

He had done what the articulate and brilliant could never have done, he had survived five days on only his resourcefulness and his daring and his unshakable belief that sooner or later his father or someone he could trust would come along and take him home again. I could feel the relief forcing his sobs, and I cried with him, because he was there and alive and if my life ended in the next instant, all the years I had spent learning to track had been justified. I was where I should be. And I was happy and thankful to be there.

BOBCAT

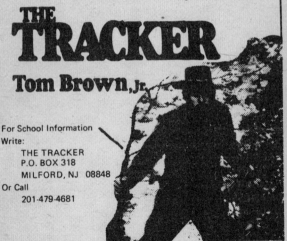